BRITAIN IN OLD PHOTOGRAPHS

KIRKBY LONSDALE
& DISTRICT

NIGEL & PHILLIP DALZIEL

SUTTON PUBLISHING LIMITED

Sutton Publishing Limited
Phoenix Mill · Thrupp · Stroud
Gloucestershire · GL5 2BU

First published 1996

Reprinted in 2002

Cover photographs: *front*: Main Street, Kirkby
Lonsdale, decorated for the arrival of HH
Princess Louise Schleswig-Holstein, 4
September 1906; *back*: Canon William
Grenside, Melling Vicarage, 1905.

British Library Cataloguing in Publication Data
A catalogue record for this book is available from the
British Library.

ISBN 0-7509-1274-X

Typeset in 10/12 Perpetua.
Typesetting and origination by
Sutton Publishing Limited.
Printed in Great Britain by
J.H. Haynes & Co. Ltd, Sparkford.

CONTENTS

Photograph of an unknown woman taken by W.H. Berry of 39 Main Street, Kirkby Lonsdale, in about 1910.

INTRODUCTION

Kirkby Lonsdale, at the junction of Westmorland, Lancashire and Yorkshire, is the chief market town of Lunesdale and set in a landscape of small villages, rolling farmland and majestic fells. Like many ancient rural communities it had always adjusted slowly to new ways. From the middle of the nineteenth century, however, the pace of social and economic change began to increase sharply and photography appeared in the area at the same time. This book, concentrating on the period from the end of the nineteenth century to the middle of the twentieth, is a record of a small north country community in transition.

At the beginning of this relatively short period of fifty to sixty years, Kirkby Lonsdale catered for all the economic, social and recreational needs of a population with traditional, narrowly defined expectations. Outside influences were beginning to be felt. Tourism had been a factor in the town economy from the early nineteenth century, but with the arrival of the railways in the 1860s increasing numbers of visitors did much to stimulate trade in the town – and not just through the purchase of postcards! By the end of the century the increased use of bicycles, the popularity of touring holidays and the availability of cheap, day rail excursions all opened the Kirkby Lonsdale district to an unprecedented tourist boom. This continued into the age of the motor car.

Changes in the nature and speed of communications disrupted the traditional pattern of local markets. Between the wars, for example, a through-train ran specially from Ingleton for Lunesdale residents to attend Kendal market. There was also a regular outflow of labour to those areas of industrial Yorkshire and Lancashire served by the railway, particularly during the period of agricultural depression at the end of the nineteenth century.

The old order, in which the landed gentry presided over an unchanging rural hierarchy, underwent a profound transformation. Local landed estates were bought by middle-class industrialists from Lancashire and Yorkshire, such as Alfred Harris of Lunefield (purchased in 1869) and Edward Lees of Thurland Castle (purchased in 1885). Established families continued in residence and outwardly much remained the same – the usual round of estate staff, rent and audit dinners, the patronage expected and given to community events and building projects, and the serious work of hunting, shooting, fishing and socializing. It was brought to an end with the two world wars and by 1945 even the greatest of the local houses, Underley Hall, had become a school.

This period of change is fortunately reflected through the eye of the lens. In 1873 *Kelly's Trade Directory* recorded nearly thirty photographers working in Cumberland and Westmorland. At first the camera was confined to the studio and made little impact on the wider locality. Early camera technology was complicated and the equipment cumbersome but by the 1880s the dry plate method (which allowed ready-prepared plates to be processed at any time after exposure) made outdoor work easier. Some of the earlier photographs in this book reflect the new sense of freedom and scope given to the studio photographer.

Landscape photography was given a further impetus by the widespread success of picture postcards, published in this country for the first time in 1894. By the turn of the century over 500 million were being posted annually at a cost of a halfpenny stamp. The efficiency of the mail service meant that people could communicate speedily and cheaply.

As photography became less of a middle-class hobby and more of a successful new industry, a wider selection of views became available. Photographers scoured the countryside recording popular attractions but also out-of-the-way landmarks, and everyday activities along with unusual or notable events. They were all required to satisfy a new travelling public and especially one caught up in the craze of postcard collecting.

Studio portraits continued to be popular for special occasions and as *carte-de-visite* for wealthier clients. In 1897 Kirkby Lonsdale boasted two resident photographers – Robert Lionel Simpson, 'artist and photographer', of 1 Jingling Lane; and Mrs E. Sutcliffe, who had a studio in New Road on the site of the present garage. By the early years of this century, however, they had departed and been replaced by a number of part-time photographers. One of these, William Henry Berry, a stationer and agent for the Provident Association of London Ltd, was recorded working at 39 Main Street in 1906 and 1910 and is known to have taken photographs in the area which he published as postcards.

A number of other Kirkby Lonsdale stationers also produced postcards. Horatio Morphet, a journeyman printer of 47 Main Street who succeeded his mother, Sarah, as a printer, bookseller and stationer in the late 1890s, was active up to the First World War. He was replaced by J. Grainger at this same address in the 1920s. Mrs Annie Moorhouse operated from 35 Main Street in the 1920s before Fred Crossley began trading from the same address in the late 1930s. Mrs Annie Willan of 10 Market Street also produced postcards after taking over from her mother, Annie Haygarth, at around the same time. There were probably more who were not listed in the directories – Scott of Kirkby Lonsdale, known to have produced work in the 1930s, remains a mystery.

The photographic trade was convenient for part-time work. Jonty Wilson, the Fairbank blacksmith, broadcaster and local historian recorded how, as an apprentice indentured to Ted Read at the Underley estate smithy, he took up photography as a means of supplementing his pay of 2s. 6d. a week. After buying a quarter-plate camera, he calculated that he would be in profit if he sold six prints for every exposure he took. His expenses included sensitized plates from the chemist for 3d. each and printed paper at 11d. for fifty sheets. During peak periods he could produce 300 photographs a week. From a marketing point of view, group photographs were understandably more profitable. Fred Towers of Town End, Main Street, also took photographs throughout Lunesdale as an adjunct to his normal work as a tailor.

Today the huge agricultural and shooting estates have largely gone and so too has the railway which brought so much change in its wake. But there is much continuity too. A strong feeling of community still exists even if the old sense of order has gone. The land is still farmed, tourism remains important and much of the attractive town and local area remains unspoiled – plenty for the modern photographer to be grateful for.

KIRKBY LONSDALE

Main Street, 27 April 1906. HRH Princess Christian of Schleswig-Holstein, who as Princess Helena was the third daughter of Queen Victoria, arrived at Kirkby Lonsdale on Friday 27 April to stay at Lunefield as the guest of the Countess of Bective. During her visit she attended the 21st Westmorland Musical Festival in Kendal and distributed prizes. The 'Welcome Arch', made of heather and foliage from Underley, was

erected by estate workmen between Richard Garlick's butcher's shop and the Waverley Temperance Hotel run by Mrs Jane Airey. Later in the year Princess Christian's daughter, Princess Louise, also visited the town. This photograph was taken by William H. Berry of 39 Main Street.

Main Street, *c.* 1907. This view, looking north to the Royal Hotel, incorporates George Duguid's cycle repair shop at No. 14 (left). By 1914 Duguid had opened a garage. Charles Wilkes stands with a customer outside his barber shop at No. 11 (right).

Town End, 1920s. This was once the edge of town, with a gate across the road to bar access to cattle. Town End House (left) stands opposite 1 Main Street, whose railings came from the enclosed garden that is now Market Square. The stone wall (right) marks the edge of the Lunefield estate.

Main Street, 1921. The building next to the Royal Hotel was redeveloped in 1897 by Alfred Harris of Lunefield and incorporates three shop frontages: No. 28 was occupied by John Brierley, cabinet-maker; No. 26, with a temporary restaurant sign hanging outside, had recently been vacated by the butcher Richard Garlick who retired in 1921; and No. 24 housed the London & Midland Bank. The Waverley Temperance Hotel, proprietor James Allsopp, stands opposite. Originally a native of Dent, Richard Garlick moved to Whittington at the age of nine in 1863. He was apprenticed to the butcher J. Stout before setting up on his own in 1876. As a tenant farmer of twenty-five acres at Harling Bank, he became greatly interested in the breeding of poultry, especially Plymouth Rocks. (see p. 47.)

Market Square, Diamond Jubilee Day, 20 June 1897. Kirkby Lonsdale turned out *en masse* for the national celebration that marked Queen Victoria's sixty years on the throne. The town band, with its conductor William Taylforth, stands in the foreground surrounded by schoolchildren. Further back are the Royal Hotel omnibus (left) and High Sheriff's State coach (right); Dr W.S. Paget-Tomlinson of The Biggins was High Sheriff of Westmorland in 1897. To the far right 'A' Company of the 2nd (Westmorland) Volunteer Battalion, the Border Regiment has turned out on parade, while the banners represent the various

Friendly Societies in the town. The building to the left of the Royal Hotel was redeveloped later in the year by Alfred Harris of Lunefield. Kirkby Lonsdale Institute, in New Road (top right), had only just been built in 1895–6. In 1897 *Kelly's Directory* listed Robert Lionel Simpson of Ivy Cottage, 1 Jingling Lane, as a Kirkby Lonsdale photographer; it is possible that this professional effort, practically on his doorstep, may be attributed to him.

Kirkby Lonsdale Institute, New Road, *c.* 1906. During the nineteenth century there was a movement to provide technical instruction to the poor and ill-educated which saw the opening of mechanics' institutes throughout the country; Kirkby Lonsdale's opened in 1854. By the end of the century this sense of mission had transformed itself into the provision of literary recreation and entertainment. The Revd John Llewelyn Davies, Vicar of Kirkby Lonsdale, was instrumental in building the Institute at the corner of New Road and Bective Road (left) in 1895. Initially it contained parish and reading rooms, but in 1896 Dr W.S. Paget-Tomlinson of The Biggins added an assembly hall in memory of his mother. This is the building to the right under the cupola. The old Mechanics' Institute struggled on until 1904 when it disbanded, presenting its 3,000-volume library to the Urban District Council. The Council used it to organize a free library at the Institute.

Market Square, which was formed out of the gardens belonging to Jackson Hall, now the Royal Hotel, seen here in about 1908. The site was purchased by public subscription in 1821 and the market, held at Kirkby Lonsdale since 1227, moved here from Market Street. Until 1932 all market dues went to the Earl of Lonsdale as Lord of the Manor. The market cross, erected in 1905 by the Revd John Llewelyn Davies, was intended to shelter the traders, as seen here. The Royal Hotel was well known for hiring out coaches and John Wilman, the owner, saw to it that the carriages were thoroughly cleaned after every trip. Two of his charabancs, which carried sixteen passengers each, wait in the square. Royal Hotel coachmen were paid a small wage which was supplemented by a percentage of the fares they collected. At the far end of the square stands the Trustee Savings Bank, founded in 1818, which was built by Thompson & Webster of Kendal on the site of Jackson Hall's kitchen gardens in 1847. On the far left is the chemist's shop run by John Bayliff, son of the builder William Bayliff of 33 New Road, until just before the start of the First World War. W.H. Berry of 39 Main Street photographed the scene.

Coronation Day parade, 22 June 1911. The coronation of King George V was marked by a public holiday and day of national celebration. In Kirkby Lonsdale a parade was organized to start at Fairbank at 10 a.m., including representatives of the Urban District Council, the Territorials, Cadet Corps, boy scouts, friendly societies with banners, children from the grammar and national schools and the town band under the direction of William Taylforth. The *Westmorland Gazette* reported that it was a blustery day with occasional showers, but this did not in any way deter the townspeople and villagers who crowded into town to enjoy the spectacle. With a flag bearer at its head, the parade moved off down Main Street to Market Square, at which point this photograph was taken, just as a dray bearing girls from the grammar school passed the Royal Hotel. Arriving at Leyfield, everyone retraced their steps to the parish church for a service which included a sermon by the vicar, the Revd Edward Askwith. Afterwards the procession continued via Mitchelgate and New Road to Market Square where more photographs were taken and the national anthem sung.

Grammar school float, Coronation Day, 22 June 1911. As part of the Kirkby Lonsdale celebrations to mark the coronation of King George V a parade was organized which, according to the *Westmorland Gazette*, included 'drays drawing pupils from the grammar school representing various characters having a reference to the Empire'. The girls, representing Victoria, New South Wales, New Zealand, Canada, India, Malta and Jamaica, sit on a dray bearing the inscription 'Lady Henry Bentinck, Underley Park Farm'. The Underley estate, as the major landowner in the area, always played a central role in community events. Girls were admitted to the grammar school for the first time in 1905.

National School float, Coronation Day, 22 June 1911. This patriotically decorated wagon carried infants from the national school in Fairbank. The school was built in 1858 to accommodate 140 boys, 140 girls and 120 infants and was enlarged in 1895. One of its first pupils, John Taylforth, returned to become headmaster from 1880 to 1918. As a member of the Kirkby Lonsdale Urban District Council (from 1907 to 1928), his place in the procession was already settled and he would have been walking in the company of fellow councillors. Both he and his brother William (director of the town band) are included in the photograph of the Kirkby Lonsdale Bowling Club (see p. 47). The children would have had a tiring day, but when they finally reached Market Square they were all presented with a coronation mug by John Wilman, owner of the Royal Hotel. At 2 p.m., in much brighter weather, sports were held on Robraine field followed by tea for all. In the evening a bonfire was lit on Casterton Fell, courtesy of Lord and Lady Henry Cavendish-Bentinck of Underley.

Market Square and the Royal Hotel, *c.* 1912. The Royal Hotel, with its eighteenth-century façade, was once a private house called Jackson Hall. Directly to the right stood the Rose & Crown Inn. On 6 December 1820 it was destroyed by a fire which also killed five maids – their memorial is in the churchyard. A public subscription enabled Hannah Roper, the landlady, to buy Jackson Hall and continue trading under the old Rose & Crown name. The purchase also allowed the townspeople to open up Market Square on the site of Jackson Hall's gardens and to build New Road over the ruins of the old Rose & Crown. Effectively Kirkby Lonsdale's first bypass, it ran from the square (on the other side of the market cross in this photograph) to the top of Mitchelgate, previously the main road to Kendal. On 23 July 1840 Queen Adelaide, widow of King William IV, paid an unexpected visit to Kirkby Lonsdale. She stayed for one night at the Rose & Crown, en route to the Lakes, in room No. 10, making use of the central balcony to greet the crowds who flocked to see her. Ever since, the inn has been known as the Royal Hotel. Notice the hotel's station wagon which carried passengers to and from Kirkby Lonsdale or Arkholme stations.

Royal Hotel indoor staff, 1920s. The hotel was a major employer throughout the nineteenth and early twentieth centuries, illustrating the importance of Kirkby Lonsdale's strategic position on the main road between Yorkshire and the Lakes and the growing impact of tourism in the area. As a coaching inn it provided a service to the town in operating connecting services to the London & North Western Railway's Kirkby Lonsdale station from 1861, and the Furness and Midland's Arkholme station from 1867. It also ran a shuttle service to the seaside at Morecambe, and to Kendal and Windermere, keeping fresh horses stabled at each terminus for the return journey. The hotel had stabling for sixty-two horses, regularly feeding and resting visitors' mounts, especially on market day. All this activity required large numbers of coachmen and stable lads. Equally important were the indoor staff. The hotel provided the best accommodation in town and catered for a wide variety of social occasions. These included rent audit dinners and annual staff dinners for the large local estates such as Underley and The Biggins, and the prestigious Lunesdale Gun Club Ball. Alice, John Wilman's sister, was the chef here until, at the age of forty-nine, she hanged herself in her bedroom in the family's lodgings. Second from the right in this photograph is Jimmy Howard, bootboy, who rose to be head waiter and retired in his seventies.

Waverley Café, 1 Market Square, *c.* 1925. The café is sited on the south side of Market Square in what was originally a range of speculative houses built shortly after the square was laid out in 1821. Pearson & Pearson, solicitors and estate agents, have occupied the east end of the row since 1918. The café was also a temperance hotel, run by Mrs Mary Jane Airey and her daughters Isabel and May until just before the First World War when it was taken over by James Midgeley. Sometime after the war it was managed by James Allsopp who handed it over to Albert Allsopp. The gentleman posing with his car is somewhat indiscriminate in his choice of locations, appearing on the next page in front of the Royal Hotel. Bicycles had made large numbers of people mobile by the turn of the century and touring holidays became popular. The Royal Hotel specifically catered for cyclists until about 1906, when the more widespread use of the motor car prompted it to diversify further and give up its CTC (Cyclists' Touring Club) connection in favour of the AA. The CTC sign, formerly on the Royal Hotel façade, is now seen on the Waverley Temperance Hotel which provided storage for bicycles. On the far left is Mary Willan's sweet shop.

Royal Hotel, *c.* 1925. From 1906 John Wilman provided garaging and petrol for motor cars. The Royal Hotel's hire business gradually converted to motor transport and by 1930 only a small number of horse-drawn vehicles were available. The Underley estate regularly hired cars here from 1910. The Royal Hotel extension (right) was added in 1822 on part of the old Rose & Crown site.

Market Square, *c.* 1930. The market cross was presented to the town by the Revd John Llewelyn Davies, Vicar of Kirkby Lonsdale 1889–1908, on Saturday 25 February 1905 – the day before his seventy-ninth birthday. Built of Morley stone and designed by John F. Curwen of Kendal, it commemorated the Llewelyn Davies family's connection with the town. At the bus stop is a joint West Yorkshire/Ribble service from Leeds to Keswick.

Market Square, *c.* 1935. By this date the great increase in motor traffic had turned the square into a car park, requiring AA signs to direct traffic around the market cross. Walter Pattison now runs the chemist's shop at the corner of Main Street (left) and Robert H. Goad's grocery shop can be seen through the arches of the cross.

Market Square, *c.* 1950. In about 1948 the authorities decided that the upper part of the market cross was unsafe. Consequently, the eight ogee ribs that held the central cross aloft were removed. The chemist's shop was now under the management of H.E.M. Evans. The railings in front of the Royal Hotel, taken away during the war, had been replaced by a low wall.

Main Street, *c.* 1902. This view from Market Square looking north up Main Street was taken before the market cross was built in 1905 (right) and the loss of the town's iron railings. One constant factor in the town scene has been Pailthorp's jewellers (left) on the corner of New Road and Main Street, still in the same location today.

Main Street, *c.* 1904. On the right is the Green Dragon – now unfortunately renamed the Snooty Fox – owned by John Wilman of the Royal Hotel. Here in 1847 William Sturgeon, scientist and inventor of the electromagnet, gave a course of lectures on electricity and optics. He was born at Whittington and returned to live at Low Biggins in 1846 before leaving for Manchester in 1850.

Main Street, 4 September 1906. HH Princess Louise of Schleswig-Holstein, daughter of Princess Christian and granddaughter of Queen Victoria, visited Kirkby Lonsdale to open a bazaar organized by the Countess of Bective in aid of the Queen Elizabeth Grammar School extension fund. The 1902 Education Act had made county education authorities responsible for the universal provision of secondary education and Westmorland County Council was developing the independent grammar school to provide for children in the area. This photograph was taken by W.H. Berry.

Main Street, *c.* 1920. This is Kirkby Lonsdale on a workday. Further down the street, what looks like window cleaning is in progress. It could also have been employees of the Kirkby Lonsdale Gas Company, established in about 1854 to supply the town from its gasometer at the bottom of Mill Brow, checking and cleaning the street lamps.

Main Street, *c.* 1904. On the right is the façade of the market house, which stands at the corner of Main Street and Market Street. Built in 1854 by a joint-stock company for £2,000, it housed a number of public rooms on the first floor and a weekly corn market on the ground floor. A public hall at the rear seated 300 for concerts and public meetings.

Main Street, *c.* 1920. John Leighton's shoemaker's shop is on the extreme left next door to the Red Dragon whose landlord, William Brunskill, left shortly afterwards. The firm of John Dean, across the road at No. 68 (far right), was managed after his father's death in 1910 by Herbert Dean, 'grocer, seed merchant and Italian warehouseman' (see p. 56). Traders relied on the custom of the local estates to a large extent. Underley Hall, for one, purchased most of its food in the town. Considering that it had to feed seventy staff, residents and up to twenty-four guests at a time, with their own complement of servants, the economic impact was significant. William Taylforth was the first manager of the Bank of Liverpool, which expanded next door into Dean's premises after its move further down the street. The motor car parked on the left bears an early Westmorland registration plate: EC76.

The Old Cross, Kirkby Lonsdale.

Horsemarket, *c.* 1930. The county police
station, built by Alfred Harris of Lunefield in
1880, stands on the corner of Horsemarket –
the site of annual horse and cattle fairs. Fodder
was stored in the low, gated arch and
conveniently passed through to the police horse
stabled behind. The building also housed a
magistrate's court (the monthly county court
was held in the market house) and
accommodation for the police sergeant.
Alexander Pearson, clerk to the Kirkby
Lonsdale justices, used to complain of the 'icy'
conditions in the building, but it would have
been nothing to what the sergeant had to
endure.

Swinemarket, 1930s. The medieval market cross, removed from the junction of Market Street and Main
Street in 1819, is capped by a seventeenth-century ball finial. In the foreground a line of flagstones covers
the beck which runs down Market Street and Mill Brow into the river.

Market St.,
Kirkby Lonsdale

Market Street, *c.* 1912. Together with Horsemarket and Swinemarket this was the town's market-place until the square was opened for trading in 1822. On the far right, at No. 9, is the working men's club. The delivery boy stands outside John Hartley's shop, advertised as a 'family grocer and seedsman, tea and coffee merchant and Italian warehouseman'. Next door at No. 15 is Gilbert Preston, watchmaker. Finally, at the end of the street is Thornborrow's 1*d.* 3½*d.* and 6½*d.* Bazaar which belonged to Thomas Robinson Thornborrow, a joiner of Kings Arms Yard. Dick Harrison's butcher's shop occupies 69 Main Street, in front of which stood the old market cross with the town lock-up at its foot. The site was found to be cramped as early as 1819 and the cross removed to Swinemarket. To the far left is the Sun Inn. The lady in the doorway of the shop further along on the left is Mrs Annie Haygarth, stationer. Next door to her at No. 12 is Thomas Lupton, cabinet-maker, followed by Miss Jane Hodgson, confectioner at No. 14. Finally, in the building standing forward of the rest, with the gas lamp outside, is Robert Richardson's butcher's shop (see p. 31).

Market Street, 1920s. On the left is the King's Arms Inn, once a house of the Carus family, whose landlord was Thomas Moss throughout most of the 1920s and '30s. Edward Richardson, bootmaker, occupied No. 8 on the far right. The Sun Inn, landlord Robert Blain, stands on the corner of Church Street opposite Richard Wilding's tobacconist's shop, itself next to Henry Dale's butcher's shop at No. 2. Beck Head House at the end of the street was once the eighteenth-century Fountain Inn rebuilt as a private house by William Carus (whose son the Revd William Carus-Wilson, founder of the Clergy Daughters' School, was born here in 1791). From 1843 it was part of the Underley Estate, Francis Pearson and John Picard both practising as solicitors from this address. From 1934 it was occupied by Mrs Wilson, district nurse and wife of Jonty Wilson the Fairbank blacksmith, and run as a nursing home which she renamed Fountain House. Part of the Urban District Council's offices can be seen to the right. The eponymous beck runs from Fountain House along Market Street and Mill Brow into the Lune, and until the 1870s was uncovered. Water could still be drawn from it in the early 1920s, through a trap door set into the road outside the Sun Inn.

Robert Richardson, butcher, pre-1914. Richardson set up as a butcher at 18 Market Street in about 1906. By 1925 Thomas Septimus Richardson was listed at this address, followed in the 1930s by Edward Birkett Richardson. Robert Richardson is seen here on his rounds among the surrounding villages.

Group photograph, 1930s. Taken in King's Arms Yard, at the rear of the inn, by 'Scott of Kirkby Lonsdale', this photograph records an event possibly connected with the working men's club next door at 9 Market Street. The passageway (left), down the side of the King's Arms, affords a glimpse of Henry Dale's butcher's shop at 2 Market Street.

Mitchelgate, pre-1914. This photograph was taken at the top of Mitchelgate facing downhill to Beck Head, with a view across to Casterton Fell. For centuries the main road out of town to the west, it was superseded in 1821 by the building of New Road.

Cressbrook, pre-1914. Built in 1849 on the Kendal road beyond Mitchelgate, Cressbrook was the property of Oliver Procter-Gregg (see p. 47), formerly of Brant Howe in Fairbank. It was known locally as 'Rogues Hall' – a name derived from the cabal of Procter-Gregg, Francis Pearson of Brant Howe and John Picard of Beck Head House, who used to meet privately before the war to decide the town's affairs. After the war it became a boys preparatory school under Felix Dowson, but is now Cedar House School.

The grammar school, *c*. 1935. Founded in 1591, it moved from Mill Brow to Biggins Lane in 1850. The main building, Springfield House, was built by George Webster in 1846 as accommodation for the headmaster and boarders. Since 1979 it has been a comprehensive school and expanded across the fields to the left.

Smithy Field, 1920s. On the extreme left is the rear of Fairbank Smithy, operated from 1921 to 1961 by Jonty Wilson. Behind rises The Gables, home to the Underley agent, Frederick Punchard and his wife Constance Holme, the novelist. To the far right stands the 1834 Wesleyan Methodist Chapel. Smithy Field is now a housing estate.

Fairbank, 1903, from the churchyard gates which were made by John Jackson (known as 'General' Jackson after the American Confederate soldier), son of the Fairbank blacksmith William Jackson who had himself made the Church Street gates in 1823. John's son, Henry, who was apprenticed in 1874, in turn made the churchyard railings. John Warbrick Smith Jackson, Henry's brother, was the last of the family to work from Fairbank smithy (at the far end of the street on the left, beyond the coach driver) in 1921. The windows in the top right corner of this photograph belong to the house where Brigadier-General Louis Wyatt lived. As GOC British troops in France and Flanders during 1920 it was his job to choose which unidentified soldier's body was to be sent for burial in Westminster Abbey as the 'Unknown Soldier'. Further along Fairbank, on the right, is the Fleece Inn, whose landlord was Richard Knowles. At the far end of the street stands Brant Howe, formerly the home of Oliver Procter-Gregg (see p. 47) but by this time the residence of Francis Pearson, solicitor cousin of Alexander Pearson and heir to Storrs Hall, Arkholme. He died on active service on 6 February 1917 while serving as a Captain in the Loyal North Lancashire Regiment.

Church gates, *c.* 1925. William Jackson of Tunstall made these gates at his Fairbank smithy in 1823. They were adapted for gas lighting and were further altered in the 1930s when Kirkby Lonsdale was connected to the national grid. The Sun Hotel, in a quiet corner overlooking the churchyard, was one of many such establishments in town to have catered for tourists for well over 150 years. Throughout the 1920s the landlord was Robert Blain.

Norman west door, pre-1914. Early publishers of postcards were fond of issuing this view. The verger is posed picturesquely against the late twelfth-century doorway which was given new pillar shafts and oak doors in the 1866–8 restoration.

St Mary's Churchyard, c. 1930. The war memorial, built by William Bayliff and designed by Austin & Paley, commemorates the forty-nine men of the parish killed in the First World War. It stands on a raised area in the churchyard, previously a stagnant pool, where the excavated bodies from the 1866–8 restoration were reburied. The obelisk (left) is a memorial to five maids killed in the Rose & Crown fire in 1820.

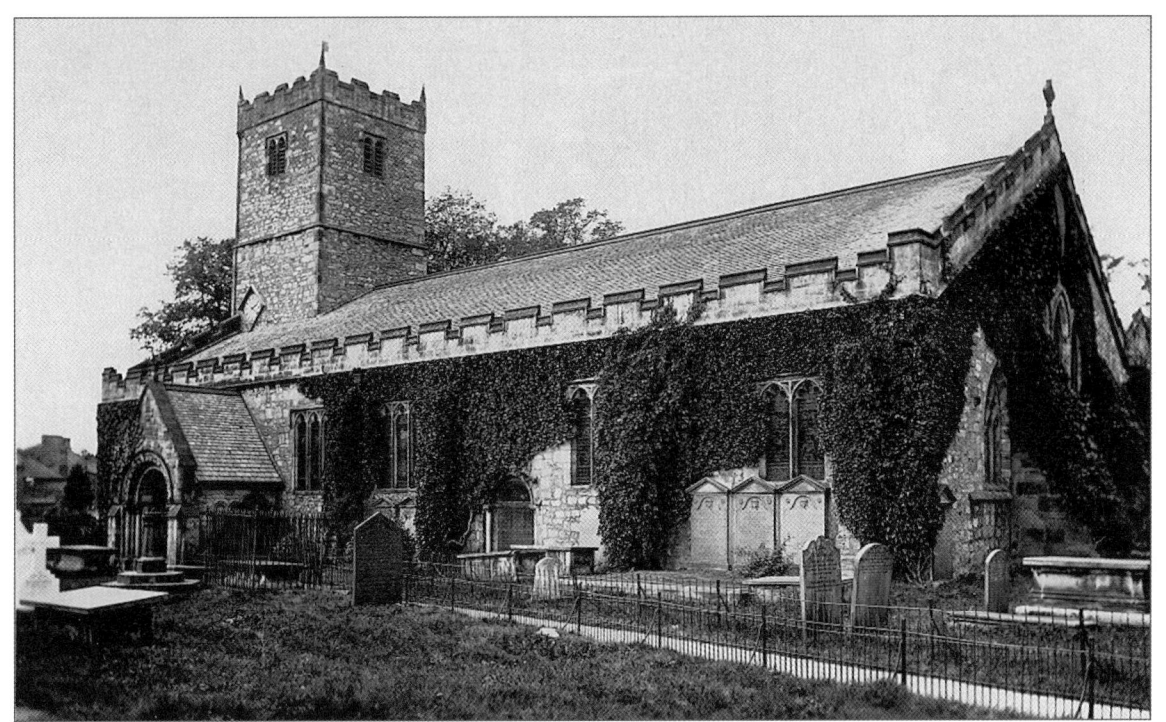

St Mary's Church, 1920s. In 1866–8 the church underwent a complete restoration costing £10,000, a sum provided by Lord Kenlis of Underley Hall in memory of his mother Amelia, Countess of Bective, who died in 1864. The Revd Henry Ware, later Bishop of Barrow-in-Furness, employed the architect E.G. Paley of Lancaster to give the church a uniform, higher-pitched roof, presumed to have been the height of an earlier Norman roof. He also added battlements and a new south porch. John Ruskin, after a visit to the town in 1875, complained of a 'fine old church . . . duly patched, botched, plastered, and primmed up; and is kept as tidy as a new pin. For your English clergyman keeps his own stage properties nowadays, as carefully as a poor actress her silk stockings'. The Victorian church railings were supposed to help keep the town children from playing among the gravestones; fighting and football were common occurrences in the nineteenth century and the cause of frequent complaints by the vicar of the day. All the railings were removed during the Second World War.

St Mary's nave and choir, 1920s. The first two piers on the left date from around 1100, possibly worked by stonemasons from Durham Cathedral. The 1866–8 restoration removed the box pews, reduced the 1619 three-decker pulpit to its present size and replaced the pillar, third from the left, removed in 1806 to allow a better view of the pulpit.

St Mary's, north aisle, *c.* 1910. An oak-beamed roof was added in 1866, replacing the flat plaster ceiling of the eighteenth century. The memorial stone above the door (right) commemorates self-taught scientist William Sturgeon (1738–1850) of Whittington.

The Vicarage, 1908. Overlooking the churchyard, the vicarage was built in 1783 by the Revd Marwood Place. The upper storey was added sometime in the 1850s by the Revd John Fisher to accommodate his pupils. Unfortunately, the overall effect was to turn a Georgian house into a Swiss cottage. In 1958 the Parochial Church Council was advised to fell the avenue of limes leading across the churchyard to the vicarage which had originally been planted in about 1737. This photograph was taken in the year the Revd John Llewelyn Davies retired after serving nineteen years as vicar. A distinguished classics scholar and Chaplain to the Queen, he was also a founder of the Working Men's College in 1854 and a Principal of Queen's College, London, which had been founded for the better education of women. His family was equally talented. Bertrand Russell, the philosopher, visited the vicarage as the friend of his two youngest sons Crompton and Theodore. His grandson, Peter Llewelyn Davies, was the inspiration for J.M. Barrie's *Peter Pan*. In 1895 his wife Mary died; she is buried to the left of this path, alongside her son Theodore who drowned in Leck Beck in 1905 aged thirty-four.

Remembrance Day service, 1932. This ecumenical service for the fallen of the First World War was organized annually by the Urban District Council. As reported in the *Westmorland Gazette*, the vicar, the Revd Robert Brown, had refused for many years to allow a service to be conducted in the churchyard by anyone but himself. The congregation is therefore led by the Methodist and Congregational ministers in Queen's Square, on the opposite side of the churchyard railings to the war memorial. They stand on a small dais to the left. The vicar is not present. Afterwards the British Legion and representatives of public bodies laid wreaths on the memorial. Behind the congregation is the shadowy form of the fountain, 'erected by public subscription gratefully to record the restoration of the parish church by Lord Kenlis AD 1868'.

Old Lunefield House from the east, before 1869. In 1812 Roger Carus bought Lunefield Estate on the edge of Kirkby Lonsdale, and by 1815 had built this neo-classical house overlooking the River Lune. It bears similarities to Casterton and Leck Halls, both the work of the architect John Webb. Canon Carus sold the house in 1869 to Alfred Harris, who demolished it and built a replacement 50 yards to the north up the bank on the right. The drive to the Carus house approached from across the low-level park to the left, leaving the main road near Devil's Bridge. Jingling Lane acted as the service road into town. It is said that the name derived from the jingling harness of Miss Carus' pony and trap passing over the concealed town drain. After 1869 a new entrance was created at Town End, the gateposts bearing the legend 'Quies Sanus', allowing the drive to make its way to the house across a bridge over Back Lane.

Lunefield from the south, *c.* 1929. Alfred Harris, a retired banker from Bingley, employed Alfred Waterhouse, known for his use of a free picturesque Gothic style, to design a replacement for the old Lunefield; this was built in 1869–70. The architect, who began his practice in Manchester, was also engaged at this time in building Manchester town hall to his winning competition design. The Harris family became active in the life of the town, especially in the formation of a school of handicrafts, which provided vocational training for sixty students in the old Inghamite and Sandemanian Chapel in Chapel Lane. Alfred Harris sold Lunefield to the Countess of Bective in 1899 and went to live in Surrey.

The Countess of Bective (right) and Constance Holme (seated), *c.* 1908. Lady Bective (1842–1928), the only daughter of the 4th Marquis of Downshire, married Lord Kenlis – later Earl of Bective and MP for Westmorland (1870–92) – in 1867 and lived at Underley until her husband's death in 1893. Constance Holme (1880–1955) was born in Milnthorpe, the daughter of a land agent. Between the wars she became a success as the author of several novels with a Westmorland setting. In 1916 she married Frederick Burt Punchard, who succeeded his father as agent to the Underley Estate, and lived at The Gables in Fairbank.

Lunefield from the west, *c.* 1934. Lady Bective lived here from 1899 as the widowed mother of Lady Henry Cavendish-Bentinck of Underley. Her London residence was at 29 Eaton Place, where she died in 1928. A strong and formidable character, she struck the townspeople as 'autocratic'. Socially well connected, she presided over house parties which included Herbert Asquith, the Liberal prime minister. However, this did not prevent her from strongly supporting the Conservative interest and she was President of their County Association, Kirkby Lonsdale District and Women's Unionist branches. In fact she joined, if not chaired, almost every local committee of note. She is buried beside her husband in Kirkby Lonsdale churchyard.

Lunefield gardens from the south, *c.* 1934. After Lady Bective's death in 1928 the house was purchased by the Co-operative Holiday Association. The Italian gardens, somewhat overgrown by this stage, extended across the site formerly occupied by the old Lunefield House.

The common room, Lunefield, 1930s. The Co-operative Holiday Association maintained the house as a holiday home except for a period during the war when it was occupied by the Royal Engineers. The window above the fireplace can be seen in the previous photograph below the right-hand chimney. Lunefield was demolished in 1959 and the site is now occupied by a housing estate.

Lunesdale Gun Club, *c.* 1895. Back row, left to right: Col Foster of Hornby Castle; William James Wilson of High Park, Oxenholme, brother of Kit Wilson of Rigmaden; William Middleton Moore of Grimeshill, Middleton; Robert Edward Fenwick of Burrow Hall; William Hollins, Barbon; Col Hargreaves of Whalley Abbey, Clitheroe; Lord Henry Cavendish-Bentinck of Underley Hall; T. Fenwick Fenwick of Burrow Hall; Charles Morley Saunders of Wennington Hall; Gerard Elyetson Thompson of Stobars Hall, Kirkby Stephen. Front row: G. Braithwaite Wilson; Col Edward Brown Lees of Thurland Castle; Capt Curteis; Capt. H.B. Rhodes of Barrock Park, Carlisle; Thomas Fawcett Warden of Lowfields, Kirkby Lonsdale; Capt H. Garnett of Wyreside, Lancaster; Myles Kennedy of Stone Cross, Ulverston.

Kirkby Lonsdale Bowling Club, *c.* 1897. Back row, left to right: Frederick Punchard, Underley Estate land agent; Oliver Procter, landowner, of Brant Howe, Fairbank; Belle Lodge, waitress; John Dean, grocer and seedsman, 68 Main Street; May Wilman, waitress; C.E. Mumford, retired businessman; Adam Slack, head gamekeeper, Underley. Middle row: Charles Bates Punchard, land agent's assistant, son of Frederick Punchard and honorary secretary of the Bowling Club; George Webster, solicitor and branch manager for the Bank of Liverpool, 66 Main Street; John Roper, solicitor; William Hodgson Bland, proprietor of the Red Dragon, 59 Main Street; John Greenbank, solicitor's managing clerk, secretary to the Gas Company and Kirkby Lonsdale market house and public buildings company; T Mattinson, greengrocer; Dr William Edward Ledgard, surgeon, 16 Main Street; John Wilman, proprietor of the Royal Hotel and Green Dragon, Main Street; John Taylforth, headmaster of the National School and an organist and director of the Choral Society; William Taylforth, solicitor's managing clerk, brother of John Taylforth; Anthony Gibson, saddler. Front row: J. Alleyne Robinson, estate agent's assistant; George Sinclair Tatham, solicitor, 6 Beck Head; J.K. Robinson, estate agent's assistant; Thomas Morton Rallinshaw, coal merchant, 1 Main Street; E.H. Tiptaft, estate agent's assistant; Richard Garlick, butcher, 7 Market Square; Leonard Hodge, hairdresser and tobacconist, 11 Main Street.

'A' Company and band of the 2nd Volunteer Battalion of the Border Regiment photographed in full dress uniform at Kirkby Lonsdale, *c.* 1890. Authorization was given to raise volunteer forces in 1859 during a periodic scare about Britain's vulnerability to invasion from France. They remained an important feature of Victorian society. During the 1890s 'A' Company was based at the Armoury, Jingling Lane, before moving to the drill hall, Beck Head. The reason why these men were on parade is not known. It could have been a routine event during one of the regular camps for volunteers which took place nearby or even something as notable as Queen Victoria's golden jubilee celebrations in 1887.

Boy's Cadet Corps, *c.* 1906. The *Westmorland Gazette*'s 1916 obituary of the Revd John Llewelyn Davies, Vicar of Kirkby Lonsdale (1889–1908), recorded that, 'Towards the close of the South African War [the Boer War of 1899–1902] he brought about the formation of a cadet company for boys and youths which has continued to flourish up to the present time, and has formed a valuable nursery from which young men have been drawn into the Territorial and other forces. This was the first cadet company in the county'. Llewelyn Davies' curate, the Revd William Charles Bertie Williams, was a Lieutenant in the 2nd (Westmorland) Volunteer Battalion of the Border Regiment based at the drill hall, Beck Head, and had responsibility for the Cadet Corps. This photograph shows him (right foreground) with his charges in full patriotic display aboard a cart belonging to William Hodgson. Possibly the driver is Hodgson himself, who first started work as a carrier to Lancaster and Kirkby Lonsdale, but by the turn of the century had replaced his mother, Fanny Hodgson, as the grocer, butter and egg dealer of Cross House, Whittington.

24 Hours Camp of North Lancs. Inf. Brigade.
Owing to Mobilisation. Kirkby Lonsdale. Aug.3rd

The twenty-four-hour camp, Kirkby Lonsdale. The North Lancashire Infantry Brigade comprised the 4th and 5th Battalions of the King's Own Regiment and the 4th and 5th Battalions of the Loyal North Lancashire Regiment. The King's Own were fond of Kirkby Lonsdale as the location of their annual summer camp, the 4th Battalion arriving from Furness and the 5th Battalion from Lancaster. The camp lasted only twenty-four hours, however, owing to the outbreak of war with Germany on 4 August 1914 and the consequent mobilization. The 5th Battalion was posted to Barrow-in-Furness for a week to guard the docks and returned to Lancaster before leaving for Didcot on 14 August. The photographer, A.G. Price of Hereford, travelled long distances to compile a whole series of presumably lucrative army photographs.

RIVER LUNE

The 'Great Frost', 1895. The *Westmorland Gazette* noted that it had been cold since the previous Christmas, but with a sudden drop in temperature in February almost the entire length of the River Lune froze over. Nothing like it had been known in living memory. An ice carnival was proposed, featuring sports and festivities, to be held on Wednesday the 14th at Devil's Bridge. Being a half-day holiday in Kirkby Lonsdale most of the town's population, and that of the nearby villages, was present. The town band played dance music under the direction of William Taylforth and prizes were awarded in speed and fancy skating, steeplechasing and hockey. Because of fading light the races were resumed the following Saturday and finished with a torchlight procession. The figure on the right, in a checked suit with his back to the photographer, is Frank Pearson, Kirkby Lonsdale solicitor and cousin of Alexander Pearson, author of *The Annals of Kirkby Lonsdale*, and grandson of that other Frank Pearson, the 'Kirkby Devil', so called because of his eloquence as a lawyer. He inherited Storrs Hall from his father in 1910 but, as a captain in the Loyal North Lancashire Regiment, died in the First World War in 1917.

Kirkby Lonsdale from the south-east, *c.* 1903. This view, seen from just across the Lancashire border, with the Tunstall road in the foreground, includes Albert Harris' now demolished Lunefield (top right). Before 1820 the main Skipton to Kendal road passed directly through the centre of Kirkby Lonsdale . Having crossed Devil's Bridge it turned right, following the river upstream before entering the town by way of Mill Brow. It continued up Market Street and Mitchelgate and out on to the Kendal road. This was superseded in 1820 by a new road built directly up the hill from the bridge (left) which brought traffic into town from Town End, along Main Street and up New Road. This early traffic-relief scheme remained unchanged until the construction of Stanley Bridge and Bentinck Drive in 1932.

8471   *Devil's Bridge.*
Kirkby Lonsdall.

Devil's Bridge, *c.* 1907. From 1861 the railways brought Kirkby Lonsdale within easy reach of industrial Lancashire and Yorkshire. In 1901, for example, the *Westmorland Gazette* reported the arrival of 500 trippers, 'chiefly mill hands from Oldham'. This group was typical of the new influx.

The Lune below Devil's Bridge, *c.* 1908. This view from the bridge no longer exists, for in 1932 Stanley Bridge was built to carry the new bypass across the river just above the promontory of rocks known as 'Gibraltar', which juts out from the right bank.

Devil's Bridge, 1920s. The bridge was often more appreciated for its function than its form. In 1901 R. Batty Parr of Casterton wrote to the *Westmorland Gazette* complaining of the common practice of tipping rubbish from Devil's Bridge; the waste littered the river bed and banks below. He would have complained to the district council but its employees were among the worst offenders!

Devil's Bridge, *c.* 1930. The angler is Robin Airey, chauffeur to Alexander Pearson of Abbot's Brow and later the driver of the first motorized mail van in Kirkby Lonsdale. To the left stands Herbert Dean, grocer and seedsman of 68 Main Street. The firm of John Dean was an old one in Kirkby Lonsdale, having originally been founded by Robert James, a gardener from Whittington Hall. His son William was succeeded in the 1890s by his apprentice John Dean, who himself handed over to his son Herbert in 1910. John Dean appears in the Kirkby Lonsdale Bowling Club photograph (see p. 47). On 3 November 1927 the Lune flooded, rising twenty feet to cover the lower part of the arches on Devil's Bridge and reaching as high as the elm tree branch seen here above the two men. This, by no means rare, demonstration of the force of the river helps to explain why the bridge stands so high and the town shuns the river bank.

Devil's Bridge, 1930s. Given the nature of the river in spate it was necessary for the first stone bridge – built in 1376–80 by the Abbey of St Mary in York, owner of Kirkby Lonsdale church and manor – to clear the highest floodwater. This rocky gorge was high, narrow and firm enough to provide the ideal location. The bridge possibly received its name from the fact that the wealthy abbey built it without soliciting alms, or charitable donations. Because the medieval Church taught that contributions to bridge-building brought donors spiritual benefits, any built without alms were sometimes regarded as 'Devil's bridges'. Oral tradition has it that an old woman, wishing to cross the swollen river to market, made a bargain with the Devil: he would build a bridge in return for the soul of the first living thing to cross it. Upon completion the supposedly naïve 'Prince of Darkness' was thwarted when the woman threw a bannock across the bridge which her dog ran to retrieve! Souls have more often been snatched by drowning in the deep pool beneath the bridge, where boys from the town have always come to swim. A nineteen-year-old Italian known as John Smith drowned here in 1869. He may have been one of the Italian workers installing the Revd Henry Ware's mosaic and alabaster reredos in the church.

Devil's Bridge and Stanley Bridge (beyond), 1950s. The narrow medieval bridge could not be made to carry modern levels of traffic. On 3 December 1932 Oliver Stanley, MP for Westmorland and Under Secretary for Home Affairs, opened a new bridge named after himself. Made of reinforced concrete and costing £21,446, it crossed the Lune in a single span of 110 ft. Devil's Bridge was subsequently pedestrianized.

Lunesdale from Robraine, 1950s. The fifty-foot wide concrete decking of Stanley Bridge, on the right, carried a new road to the south of Devil's Bridge and Kirkby Lonsdale. This bypass was opened by Lady Henry Cavendish-Bentinck on 3 December 1932 and named Bentinck Drive in memory of her late

The Lune Valley with Barbon Fell behind, taken from the new bypass, *c.* 1955. Kirkby Lonsdale is the market town for a wide area and situated at a strategic crossroads. Behind and above the church (left) is Underley Hall, through the trees. To the far right can be seen Lunefield's tower, demolished in 1959.

Ruskin's View, *c.* 1930. In 1816 J.M.W. Turner visited Kirkby Lonsdale and sketched the Lune Valley from the churchyard, which he finally painted in 1817–18. John Ruskin, art critic and champion of Turner, praised this view in 1875 as 'one of the loveliest scenes in England – therefore, in the world'. It has since been known as 'Ruskin's View'.

Ruskin's View, *c.* 1950, sometimes known as 'Surprise View' owing to the heavily wooded nature of Church Brow from which this photograph was taken. Formerly part of the vicarage glebe land, it was purchased by Alexander Pearson and given to the parish council in 1947.

Ruskin's View, *c.* 1955. Ruskin made people think about the value of such prospects at a time when, in 1875, he was complaining that the townsfolk 'go through the churchyard to the path on the hill-brow, making the new iron railing an excuse to pitch their dust-heaps, and whatever of worse they have to get rid of, crockery and the rest, – *down over the fence* among the primroses and violets to the river, – and the whole blessed shore underneath, rough sandstone rock throwing the deep water off into eddies among shingle, is one waste of filth, town-drainage, broken saucepans, tannin, and mill-refuse', *Fors Clavigera.*

NORTH LUNESDALE

Lord Henry Cavendish-Bentinck (1863–1931), 1927. He was step-brother of the 7th Duke of Portland and Conservative MP for West Norfolk (1886–92) and South Nottingham (1895–1906 and 1910–29). Regarded by Alexander Pearson as 'a magnificent specimen of an English country gentleman' he was much liked in the locality, devoting himself to public service, improving the Underley estates and serving as Lord Lieutenant of Westmorland (1926–31) and on the county council. Perhaps surprisingly, he was also an enthusiastic art collector, the first chairman of the Contemporary Art Society and a patron of British artists. His sister, Lady Ottoline Morrell, was the famous Bloomsbury hostess. On the liberal wing of his party, he gave support to its younger MPs including Harold Macmillan, the future prime minister.

Lady Henry Cavendish-Bentinck (1869–1939), *c.* 1920. She was born Lady Olivia Taylour, the only surviving child of Thomas, Earl of Bective, and married Lord Henry Cavendish-Bentinck in 1892. At her father's death the following year she inherited a life interest in the 25,000 acre Underley Estate in Westmorland, Lonsdale and Deeside. It included some of the finest shooting in the country, had a staff of 163 and a rent roll of £90,000. By the standards of the day she was an enlightened employer. Her guests at Underley included Queen Mary and the Prince of Wales, later Duke of Windsor. As she had no children the estate passed to a distant cousin, Madeline Pease, at her death.

Underley Hall gates. When Thomas, Lord Kenlis, later Earl of Bective, inherited Underley from his mother in 1864 he created a new south entrance on Keastwick Road. Built together with the lodge by Paley & Austin in about 1868, it replaced the old entrance drive from Fairbank. The railings, gates and two outer piers have long since disappeared.

Underley Hall *en fête*, *c.* 1905. Lord Henry was Ruling Councillor of the Kendal Habitation of the Primrose League – a Conservative Party organization founded in 1883 – for whose benefit he hosted this garden party. The lamps on the gate piers were lit by the estate gasometer, built by Lord Bective in the 1870s for £2,512 4*s*. 2*d*. Electricity had superseded gas by 1935.

Underley Hall, *c.* 1904. The Hall stood at the centre of 173 acres of park and 56 acres of gardens. In 1893 the estate employed twenty-six gardeners, allowing Lord Henry to build a series of horticultural showpieces. As a keen botanist he financed overseas plant expeditions which returned with many rare specimens, some still flourishing at Underley today. The 'Catamaran' crossing is at the bottom of this postcard view of Underley by Horatio Morphet.

The 'Catamaran', Underley, *c.* 1900. This twin-hulled boat was constructed by Underley Estate workers to provide access to Lord Henry's 'Wild Garden' – an area of rock planted with alpines and heather – on the east bank of the Lune. The 'Catamaran' was propelled by means of a hand crank along cables stretched across the river. It carried six to eight passengers but was also used by the Underley gardeners to bring back river gravel to spread on the paths. Lord and Lady Henry regularly opened the 'Wild Garden' to the public. In 1905 the *Westmorland Gazette* noted that it was to be open without charge every Sunday afternoon during August and September, with access via Casterton Woods. The garden did not long survive the destructive power of the Lune: by the time of Lord Henry's death in 1931 two significant floods, in 1927 and 1931, had reduced the garden to nothing more than its original sand and rock. This same violence once caused a boy to be washed downstream into the 'Catamaran' cables, where he drowned.

Underley Hall south façade, c. 1910. Underley was an early example of the Jacobean revival and was built by Alexander Nowell in 1825 to the design of George Webster. Before 1914, society house parties gathered for the shooting and could number twenty-four guests, which meant eighty to ninety additional residents in the house including staff and visitors' servants. Edward VII, when Prince of Wales, came for the grouse shooting and Harold Macmillan was a regular visitor. Every year the estate reared 5,000 ducks at Terrybank Tarn and 15,000 pheasants for sport. After her husband's death Lady Henry rented out the shooting but by 1933 had ceased to employ gamekeepers.

Underley Hall, *c.* 1920. This postcard view of the east façade of Underley Hall was published by J. Grainger of 47 Main Street, Kirkby Lonsdale, and shows the original Webster-designed building to the left. Lord Bective's programme of improvements saw the addition of an 82 ft tower and the north-east wing in 1872–3 to the design of Paley & Austin, which replaced Webster's office wing. The conservatory, measuring 70 ft by 20 ft with a connecting corridor 75 ft long, was built in 1875 to the design of the same Lancaster architects. According to the Underley Improvement Account it cost £2,829 12*s.* 10*d.* The three windows of Lady Henry's bedroom are directly underneath and to the left of the clock; Lord Henry slept in the room to the right. On ground-floor level, the morning room lay behind the colonnade with the library to the right, while Lady Henry's boudoir was at the bottom of the tower.

Lady Henry at Underley Hall, *c.* 1930. Lady Henry was more interested in her dogs – elk hounds and cairns – than in Lord Henry's collection of Post-Impressionist and contemporary British art. Directly above her hangs a painting by the Bloomsbury artist Duncan Grant, of whom Lord Henry was the foremost patron.

Underley Hall, *c.* 1930. During the 1930s the estate was employing half the staff of forty years previously. In 1933 Lady Henry brought the shooting to a close but Underley remained a major employer and centre of gracious living. By 1935 electric lighting was installed, involving five miles of wiring, and in 1937 Underley was visited by Queen Mary.

Keastwick Institute in the 1930s. In 1902 Lord and Lady Henry Cavendish-Bentinck built the Keastwick Institute, 'for the use and enjoyment of those who lived on the Underley estate, in memory of Thomas, Lord Bective', Lady Henry's father. Seen here with the Men's Institute, tenants, staff and anyone else connected with the estate, Lady Henry sits with her pet elk hound. Seated to her left is William Pearson, the estate clerk of works; next to him, Tom Procter, a painter and decorator. To Lady Henry's right is Billy Procter, son of Tom, later a clerk in the offices of solicitors Pearson & Pearson; Bob Fisher and Leonard Lowe, members of the forestry staff. Tommy Howarth, on the far left of the front row, was also a forester on the estate. Lady Henry was the founder and President of the Keastwick Women's Institute, which met monthly and was the first to be established in the area.

Underley Bridge, seen here in about 1950, was built in 1872–5 by Thomas, Lord Bective to the design of Paley & Austin. It extended the north drive across the River Lune towards Barbon station, a far more convenient terminus than Kirkby Lonsdale for anyone visiting Underley. According to the Underley Improvement Account the total cost of the bridge was £13,098.

Underley Hall, *c.* 1950. After Lady Henry's death in 1939 the hall was occupied by Hordle House boys' prep school, evacuated from Bournemouth. At the end of the war it was bought by Oakfield Girls' School. By 1945 the conservatory had been dismantled, to be replaced by the unsympathetic Bishop Flynn Memorial Chapel, erected in 1964–5 during the tenure of St Michael's College Roman Catholic Junior Seminary (1959–75). Underley is now a school for boys with learning difficulties.

The Biggins, *c.* 1905. In 1889 Dr William Paget inherited The Biggins estate from a distant cousin, Elizabeth Tomlinson. In 1893 he proceeded to build a new house in the Elizabethan style to the designs of William Verity. The contractor was William Bayliff of New Road, Kirkby Lonsdale. A fire, caused by a fused electrical wire in the gunroom, engulfed the house on the evening of 31 December 1942 and the building was subsequently demolished.

Dr W.S. Paget-Tomlinson (1848–1937) in his state coach, with an escort of Javelin Men, 1897. This photograph was taken at The Biggins to record Dr Paget-Tomlinson's tenure as High Sheriff of Westmorland and shows (left to right): J. Jackson, Lane House Farm; James Kirkbride, Broomfield Farm; Isaac Bargh, Holme House Farm; Thomas Garnett, footman; D. Lawson, footman; Dr Paget-Tomlinson; T. Bristow, coachman; William Shepherd, Abbot Hall Farm; William Bayliff, builder, New Road, Kirkby Lonsdale; Thomas Hobson, Keastwick Farm. Dr Paget-Tomlinson was a prominent member of Lunesdale society with a high-Victorian sense of public duty. A physician and surgeon before inheriting The Biggins in 1889, he took the Tomlinson name and subsequently maintained a position as a gentleman landowner. Having studied at Liverpool, London, Berlin and Vienna, his medical knowledge was put to good use as chairman of various committees on Westmorland County Council. He was strongly in favour of school medical inspections and put them into practice at Queen Elizabeth Grammar School, where he was Chairman of Governors, prior to their general introduction in 1910. He was also a magistrate, Deputy Lieutenant of Westmorland and director of the church choir. As a church organist he rebuilt and enlarged the organ in 1928 and 1934.

The Biggins gardens, *c.* 1905. The rock garden was overlooked by the terrace, thought to be an exact copy of the one at Haddon Hall, Derbyshire. The house was occupied during the Second World War by Moorland School, Blackburn, and from the balcony overlooking the terrace seven children and three adults were rescued from the fire that destroyed the building.

Meathop Sanatorium, *c.* 1910. Dr W.S. Paget-Tomlinson was a joint founder and benefactor of the Meathop Sanatorium for respiratory diseases, near Grange-over-Sands, in 1900. It was one of the first such institutions in the country to be opened to the poor. In the foreground are the men's shelters.

Rigmaden, Mansergh, from the west, *c.* 1915. Designed by Websters of Kendal in the Greek Revival style and built by Christopher Wilson in 1825, the house was dismantled in about 1956 because of an outbreak of dry rot. At the time this photograph was taken it was the home of Colonel Christopher 'Kit' Wilson, a well-known local character. Famous for his Suffolk sheep, he also bred high-stepping 'Wilson' ponies – a hackney and fell pony cross – and in the 1870s experimented with a silo method of winter feed storage which he patented. He added a billiard room (left) and made Rigmaden the second north country house to be lit by electricity, in 1883. He was fascinated by technology and, unsurprisingly, became the owner of the first car in Westmorland, which bore the number plate EC1. Rigmaden sits in a commanding position overlooking the Lune Valley and its gaunt ruins were a notable feature of the area until the recent restoration which has seen the house subdivided. Interestingly, a colonnade, part of the original unexecuted Webster designs, has been built on to the south façade (right).

Terry Bank, Old Town, *c.* 1912. The old coach road from Kirkby Lonsdale to Kendal runs directly in front of this house which was built in the sixteenth century by the Conder family of Mansergh. An aggrandized farmhouse, with barns and shippons attached (right), it was rebuilt in 1846 and bears a datestone of 1910 on the south wing gable (left).

Grimeshill, Middleton, *c.* 1905. The house was built in about 1836 by William Moore to a consciously antiquarian design by George Webster of Kendal. It replaced a seventeenth-century seat of the Moores and was itself demolished in 1938. William Middleton Moore died in 1909 and was succeeded by a daughter, Ella, who married Frederick Carleton Cooper of Carleton Hall, Penrith, in 1886.

The Swan, Middleton, *c.* 1904. Standing at the heart of the scattered township of Middleton, the Swan Inn can rightly be called its social centre. William Winster was landlord here until his death in 1921. He also farmed in the area, which accounts for the barns flanking what is still obviously a farmhouse.

The seventeenth-century Middleton Bridge, seen here in about 1906, crosses the River Rawthey directly above its confluence with the Lune (seen in the middle distance). In 1911 a ferro-concrete saddle was added for strength and two concrete balconies were placed at the apex to act as stopping places. Yorkshire lies to the right and Westmorland to the left.

BARBON

Barbon station, *c.* 1913. The London & North Western Railway's Ingleton–Low Gill line was opened in 1861, serving Barbon with four stopping trains daily each way. In 1954 all regular passenger traffic was withdrawn but a special beginning- and end-of-term train for the local boarding schools (Casterton, Cressbrook, Sedbergh and Kirkby Lonsdale grammar schools) ran until 1964 when Barbon station was closed.

The Station Hotel, *c.* 1912. This photograph was taken from the station platform. It shows a fairly substantial building for a village the size of Barbon, explained, of course, by the large number of tourists arriving by train from industrial Yorkshire. At this date the landlord of the hotel was Charles Wilberforce.

War memorial, 1920s. The war memorial was unveiled in 1920 and stands at the junction of New Road and Station Road which leads past the Barbon Hotel (formerly the Station Hotel) to the station and church. The hotel landlord was Charles Henry Staples who, throughout the 1920s, advertised a garage, fishing and tennis among the establishment's attractions.

The Barbon Inn (formerly the Station Hotel and Barbon Hotel) during the 1950s. Directly ahead, past the hotel, can be seen the station buildings, now demolished, with the level crossing gates open for road traffic. The station closed on 24 April 1964, to be followed by complete closure of the line on 26 July 1966.

New Road, *c.* 1914. As district council representative the Vicar of Barbon, the Revd James Harrison, helped obtain the widening of New Road and other village improvements. In 1884 he gave the reading room, built further up New Road, to the parish. The puff of smoke in the centre of the photograph comes from a train travelling south out of the station. Barbon Manor is on the hillside to the left.

Barbon village, *c.* 1908. The Wesleyan Chapel on the right was built in 1888 and reflects the growing strength of Methodism in the area which itself prompted the rebuilding of the parish church. Further on to the left are the smithy steps. The last two buildings on the right are, respectively, the Station Hotel and station.

Station Road, *c.* 1912. The smithy steps, seen in the previous photograph from the opposite direction, are to the immediate right. How this pleased the residents of the prosperous Victorian villa next door is not known. Before the First World War the Barbon blacksmiths were Tallons, father and son. James Robinson Tallon, the son, would have been fifty-eight years old in 1912.

Barbon village, *c.* 1922. This is Barbon, looking east towards Barbon Low Fell, without the electricity substation which now stands in the corner of the field next to the road.

The Pack Horse Bridge, Beckfoot, crosses Barbon Beck upstream from the ford. It was built in 1571 probably by John Hardy of Barbon and cost 22s. 4d. At this period, around 1913, the two farms which comprise High Beckfoot on the north bank were occupied by John Willan, yeoman, and John and Joseph Winn.

Shepherd with Scotch sheep, Barbon, c. 1900. These sheep were probably gathered from the fells in about early July prior to the summer clipping. Flocks were also brought down around late February and August for dipping. Originally they were given a coating of tar to help protect against parasites, but from the mid-nineteenth century dipping became increasingly popular as an alternative and was made compulsory in 1905.

Prior to clipping, sheep were often given a good wash in a dub or deep pool such as the one here at Barbon, *c.* 1900. On hot days this job was no doubt appreciated by the men doing the work! Wet fleeces were very difficult to cut and the sheep were left to dry out thoroughly before being taken to the shearer. The ancient yearly cycle of gathering the sheep, lambing, dipping and clipping was a community enterprise. It required large numbers of helpers from among the neighbours and the local community to supplement the work of family and hired hands.

Sheep clipping, Barbon, *c.* 1900. Clipping was the most important event of the farming year in an area which concentrated on sheep farming. All hands were drafted in for this hard thirsty work and traditional farm hospitality included being plied with pints of tea and much stronger liquids! These men are sitting astride their clipping stools using hand shears; the best workers could fleece seventy to eighty sheep a day. When the work was done sports, socializing and dancing continued well into the night.

The Vicarage, *c.* 1907. It was built to house the new perpetual curate, the Revd James Harrison, in 1872 on land donated by Thomas, Lord Bective of Underley. Together with the Shuttleworths of Barbon Manor, he was the major landowner in the area. Barbon was an ancient chapelry of St Mary's, Kirkby Lonsdale, and the curacy was in the gift of its vicar.

St Bartholomew's Church from the south-east, *c.* 1925. Under the influence and direction of the Revd James Harrison the old 1815 chapel was replaced by this splendid example of a Paley, Austin & Paley-designed church in 1893. Miss Eleanor Eastman gave £1,000 to the overall cost of £3,000, the rest being raised by public subscription.

St Bartholomew's Church from the south-west, *c.* 1907. This refined example of a Paley, Austin & Paley church in the Perpendicular Gothic style displays all the hallmarks of the firm at its best. Of particular note is the massive central tower, just a little wider than nave and chancel, and the marvellous spatial development of the interior with the crossing lit from above by windows set in the tower. This postcard view was taken from Barbon station and includes a glimpse of the drive leading to Barbon Manor high up on the fellside. The tower clock was given by the Revd James Harrison to commemorate the coronation of Edward VII in 1902. Absent from this scene is the church lych-gate which was also a gift of the Revd James Harrison in 1915.

The interior of St Bartholomew's Church, *c.* 1930. The replacement of the gas lighting has been the only significant change to the interior of the church since its consecration on 9 September 1893. The organ was paid for by the Revd James Harrison and the case was made in the village, as was the chancel screen installed in 1910 in memory of the Misses Margaret and Mary Harrison.

Barbon Manor, *c.* 1902. Janet Shuttleworth, the heiress of Gawthorpe Hall whose family had owned land in Barbon since the sixteenth century, married Dr James Kay in 1842. Sir James Kay-Shuttleworth, as he became, built Barbon Manor in 1863 to the design of E.M. Barry. A somewhat suburban version of a shooting box in the French Classical style, it was sited high on Barbon Fell facing south.

Barbon Manor, *c.* 1912. Sir James Kay-Shuttleworth (1804–77), Secretary to the Committee of Council on Education 1839–49, under whose influence a system of free national education developed, retired here after his wife's death in 1872. He began his working life as a physician in Manchester, interested primarily in sanitary reform. A practical man who believed in 'the beauty of expediency', he came to see education as the means to alleviate suffering among the poor. Together with his friend Matthew Arnold, he convinced the Victorian establishment of the need for universal educational provision. Arnold was often a visitor here in the 1860s, coming for the grouse shooting. Sir James was created a baronet in 1849. His son, Sir Ughtred, was Under Secretary of State for India and created 1st Baron Shuttleworth in 1893, the year he built the west wing and tower (right) which was demolished in 1955. The original house (left) survives in a sympathetic remodelling by Claud Phillimore.

CASTERTON

Village school, Casterton, *c.* 1841. The Revd William Carus-Wilson, ever eager to improve social conditions if he could also raise the moral tone, built the village school in 1839. The upper rooms accommodated 'twelve aged poor' who were to be conducted in morning and evening prayer by the schoolmistress. Its situation by the turnpike road, and in direct view of the parsonage, perhaps accounted for 'some unnecessary ornament and expense which the peculiar situation seemed to call for'. 'Such a building', he said, 'should not cost more than £300.' The parsonage, seen behind the bridge crossing Casterton Beck, was built by Carus-Wilson in 1841 for £1,300.

National School, *c.* 1895. By now a public elementary school with an average attendance of twenty-two, the building had lost its architectural decoration and acquired outside conveniences, a coal-house and bicycle shed; the upstairs rooms were rented out. Photographed against the wall overlooking Casterton Beck are, from the right: William Hardacre, sub-postmaster and shoemaker; Elizabeth Knowles, schoolmistress; Mrs Judd, William Hardacre's sister, married to John Judd, gardener; Millie, William Hardacre's daughter. Miss Knowles was the daughter of James Knowles, joiner and landlord of the George & Dragon, now the Pheasant Inn. In the 1891 census she is listed as a thirty-year-old schoolmistress, a post she was to retain until the early 1920s. In 1972 the village school was closed, being bought by Casterton school for use as extra classrooms. The photographer must have stood in the garden of the Homestead, which was both home to the Hardcastles and village post office. The lane passing directly in front of the sitters led down to Low Wood Middle Class Boarding School for Girls. In 1840, visiting what was then the servants' school, Queen Adelaide's carriage was pulled down this lane by the villagers after one of her horses broke a trace.

Vicarage, 1920s. In 1841 the Revd William Carus-Wilson built a parsonage for the Curate and Chaplain to the Clergy Daughters' school. He described its erection as 'the most efficient augmentation which can take place after a Church is consecrated'. In 1888 Casterton became a separate parish. Since 1976 the house has been the residence of Casterton School's headteacher.

Casterton Hall, c. 1907. William Wilson Carus-Wilson, MP for Cockermouth and father of the Revd William, built this neo-classical house in 1811 to replace the older Casterton Hall of his Wilson forebears. It was probably designed by John Webb and bears marked similarities to Leck Hall and old Lunefield. By 1907 the owners were the Bickersteths from Liverpool.

The Richardson family of Fell Gate Farm, Casterton, *c.* 1903. Eleanor Garnett from Bentham in Yorkshire – married to John Richardson, a tenant farmer from Burrow in Lancashire – is seen here with six of her eight children. They are, from the left: Florence, later to emigrate to Canada; Elizabeth, who became a teacher of the violin and pianoforte; James, born in 1890, who emigrated to the mid-west states of America; the next two boys are William and Henry (it is not clear which is which, but both were to follow their elder brother in emigrating to America); and finally Doris, the youngest child, who became a missionary in Nigeria and died unmarried. The two eldest children of the family, Alfred, born in 1883, and John, born in 1887 or 1888, had left home and were working at other farms.

Holy Trinity Church, *c.* 1911, built by the Revd William Carus-Wilson in 1833 for the use of the township and 'for the perfecting of the arrangements for the Clergy Daughters' School'. It seated 480, including a school gallery for 130, and cost £750. During Queen Adelaide's visit in 1840 the *Westmorland Gazette* recorded the royal party's 'approbation as respected both its simple unpretending beauty, and the small sum for which it was erected'.

Holy Trinity Church tower, pre-1913. In 1860 a new chancel, designed by E.G. Paley of Lancaster, was added to the original structure and in 1891 a thorough restoration was undertaken. Carus-Wilson's battlemented tower was altered in about 1913 in favour of a more prosaic parapet.

Casterton village. This photograph was taken shortly after the addition of the new parapet to the church tower and shortly before the First World War. The vicarage is to the left of the church and above the post office in the lane leading to Low Wood School. The Clergy Daughters' School is beyond, and to the right of, the church.

Casterton village, 1950s. Little has changed in the intervening years. The war memorial now stands at the corner of the churchyard. With the amalgamation of the Clergy Daughters' School and Low Wood in 1921, it is Casterton School which dominates the village. On the extreme left is the Elementary School which closed in 1972.

Casterton village, 1920s. The driver of the car is probably the Revd Arnold Whately, Vicar of Casterton 1922–8. The building on the right is the church room which was given to the parish by Miss Lucy Bickersteth of Casterton Hall in 1909. She also deposited £325 with the Diocese of Carlisle, the interest to be used for its upkeep. In 1978 it became the village hall.

Casterton village, *c.* 1960. This is quite a different prospect from the photograph taken in about 1911 (top of p. 94) and yet both were taken from the same angle. Much of the tree cover has been cut back and the road widened.

Low Wood School, pre-1914. In 1820 the Revd William Carus-Wilson founded a 'School for the training of girls for servants', and later teachers, in Rose Cottage, Tunstall, where he was vicar from 1816 to 1825. Carus-Wilson's aim was to provide girls with vocational training to enable them to earn an honest living. At the time, teaching was considered not so much a profession as a trade and even governesses to wealthy households were regarded as servants, albeit superior ones. In 1837 the school moved to Casterton where 100 poor girls were clothed, lodged, boarded and educated in reading, writing, knitting, sewing and serving. By 1883 it was transformed into Low Wood Middle Class Boarding School for Girls, offering a broader education and housed in this building which had an attached sanatorium (built in 1897). Its governing body was the same as the Clergy Daughters' School.

Junior house, Casterton School, *c.* 1930. Owing to declining numbers, failing standards and a critical Board of Education report, Low Wood was forced to amalgamate with its near neighbour, the Clergy Daughters' School, in 1921. This new body was called Casterton School and the Low Wood building became the junior school under the name of Brontë House.

Casterton School front entrance (top) and west front (below), 1923. The Clergy Daughters' School moved from unhealthy and inadequate premises at Cowan Bridge to much more suitable buildings seen here, obtained by the founder, the Revd William Carus-Wilson, in 1832. As pupil numbers increased so did additions and improvements to the buildings. In 1865 a new wing was completed housing thirty dormitory cubicles and other facilities financed by a memorial trust commemorating Carus-Wilson, who had died in 1859. Casterton School has never looked back!

The elegant and spacious-looking front hall of Casterton School, 1923, was designed to impress the visitor. Appearances were not all they seemed, however. One former pupil, Miss Kate Price Jones, remembered the punishment regime in the 1830s being 'very severe', older girls being locked in the 'cage' or closet under the front hall stairs!

One of the schoolrooms at Casterton in 1923, designed for quite large numbers of pupils. The decor was invariably dark and the rooms were illuminated by gaslight from the fittings suspended from the ceiling. Gas was installed at the school in 1870 but in 1929 an electric generator was purchased for £1,715, sufficient to power 317 lights.

School hall, Casterton, 1923. Part of the improvements made at the school during the 1890s included the building of a new assembly hall to cope with growing numbers of pupils. The original school roll in 1832 numbered 104 girls and this rose to 133 in 1879. It continued to rise gradually to 164 in 1929.

The girls' sitting room, Casterton School, 1923. It may not look particularly comfortable but at least it was spacious! The original building layout in 1832 only allowed for two schoolrooms – the upper and lower. The lower, ground floor room became the girls' sitting room in 1921. The raised table suggests that the room was used for prep or some other supervised activity.

The upper schoolroom at Casterton in 1923, when it also doubled as the dining room. It continued as a schoolroom until 1956 when it was converted for use as the headmistress's flat.

Dining room, Casterton School, 1923. In the mid-1920s various improvements were suggested by the Board of Education inspectors including enlargement of the dining room, seen here in its completed state. The mention of school food may, for some of us, recall memories of soggy vegetables and tasteless semolina pudding but this splendid scene anticipates gastronomic delight!

Domestic science room, Casterton School. The subject was central to the curriculum of Low Wood which was established in 1820 to train girls for domestic service. It merged with the Clergy Daughters' School in 1921 at just the time, after the First World War, when servants were harder to find and it was apparent that they were going to be increasingly difficult to afford. Many middle-class homes were beginning to rely more on the domestic work of family members. Knowledge of the domestic arts was, in any case, useful for young ladies destined to supervise their own domestic staff. At Casterton School, therefore, there was a new emphasis on domestic science education which was increasingly popular with the parents if not the girls! Here, in 1923, the domestic science room is laid out for cookery lessons. Sewing machines are positioned under the windows to the left. At the end of the room is a 'double-decker' stove for heating dozens of flat-irons at a time.

Casterton School library, 1923. Hardly an exciting photograph displaying the cut-and-thrust of academic life at the school, but this was one of a series of postcards designed to publicize the range of facilities available to pupils. How successful it was as a marketing exercise is difficult to tell, but no doubt parents of existing pupils were reassured to know that a library existed!

The art room at Casterton School in 1923, amazingly neat and tidy and generally free of art! The school benefited from more relaxed discipline and a widening range of activities from the 1890s. Some pupils were able to attend the art school in Kirkby Lonsdale which improved the general level of drawing skills. In 1929 the old art room, above, was superseded by a new one created as part of the post-war redevelopment plan.

Cricket match, Casterton School, 1920s. In mid-Victorian times it was considered 'unladylike' and even unhealthy for women to engage in energetic sporting activity. By the 1890s this view was fading and Miss Williams, the new lady superintendent (headmistress) from 1892, encouraged the introduction of cricket at Casterton. By the 1920s it was well established and was positively encouraged, along with hockey and other sports, by Westmorland County Council which facilitated matches between schools. In 1925 the first full-time games mistress was appointed, a new gymnasium built and the playing fields upgraded, although at the time girls were charged extra for regular physical training.

Part of the school redevelopment in the 1890s included the creation of two terraced tennis courts, seen in these photographs of the 1920s, which came into use from 1897. In the redevelopment work after the First World War a new third floor was added to the 'New Building', seen before (above) and after (below), providing additional classroom space.

SOUTH LUNESDALE

The Clergy Daughters' School, Cowan Bridge; engraving, *c.* 1830. The school was founded in 1823 by the Revd William Carus-Wilson to provide girls with a 'plain and useful education'. Charlotte and Emily Brontë were pupils here but were withdrawn in 1825 during an epidemic of tuberculosis which killed their two older sisters. The school features as 'Lowood' and Carus-Wilson as 'Mr Brocklehurst' in Charlotte Brontë's *Jane Eyre*.

Park House, which stands on the west bank of Leck Beck, *c.* 1912. It was built at the end of the sixteenth century and restored in 1676 by Edward Wilson of Dallam Tower. Its name commemorates an area of detached medieval parkland formerly linked to Thurland Castle. In 1912 it was occupied by Herbert Barnes, a tenant farmer.

Cowan Bridge, *c.* 1905. The village sits astride the main road from Kirkby Lonsdale to Skipton at the point where it crosses Leck Beck. Theodore Llewelyn Davies, a promising civil servant at the Treasury and son of the vicar of Kirkby Lonsdale, drowned in the swollen stream on 25 July 1905 after hitting his head on a concealed rock at Job's Dab, a favourite family bathing place. It is possible that this photograph was taken by or for Alfred Ireland, the village sub-postmaster, who is known to have published his own postcards. It shows the heart of the village with Ireland's shop and post office to the left and a little further on the crossroads – at the point where the children stand next to the village water pump – with the road to Leck on the left and that to Burrow on the right. Cowan Bridge was in fact the nearest village to Kirkby Lonsdale station, built in 1861 on the London & North Western Railway's Ingleton–Low Gill line and closed in 1966. This road is now a main trunk road, the A65.

Cowan Bridge post office, *c.* 1920. John Ireland died during the 1880s and was succeeded at Arkholme post office by his widow, Ellen, and in his trade of shoemaker by his three sons, Alfred, Mark and Frederick. By 1898 Alfred Ireland had set himself up in Cowan Bridge as a grocer, shoemaker and sub-postmaster.

Lowood Hotel, Cowan Bridge, *c.* 1930. Between the wars the Red Lion Private Hotel became the Lowood, from the pseudonym given by Charlotte Brontë to the old Clergy Daughters' School in her novel *Jane Eyre*. The building in the distance is all that remains of the old school. Today the main road bypasses this bridge altogether.

'Lowood', *c.* 1930. By the time Mrs Gaskell came to write her *Life of Charlotte Brontë* in 1857, the Brontë literary industry was well under way. She described the old Clergy Daughters' School as 'a long, bow-windowed cottage, now divided into two dwellings. It stands facing the beck, between which and it intervenes a space, about 70 yards deep, that was once the school garden. This original house was an old dwelling of the Picard family [John Picard, the Kirkby Lonsdale solicitor, was a descendant], which they had inhabited for two generations. They sold it for school purposes and an additional building was erected, running at right angles from the older part. This new part was devoted expressly to schoolrooms, dormitories &c.; and after the school was removed to Casterton it was used for a bobbin-mill connected with the stream, where wooden reels were made out of the alders which grow profusely in such ground as that surrounding Cowan Bridge. The Mill is now destroyed. The present cottage was, at the time of which I write, occupied by the teachers' rooms, the dining-room and kitchens and some smaller "bedrooms".' The remaining part of the building had been divided into smaller cottages by 1930, but was still celebrated for its Brontë and *Jane Eyre* connections as this postcard shows.

Golder Cocker Café, Cowan Bridge, 1950s. The café was housed in a corrugated iron shed by the side of the main road through the village. It took advantage of the passing motor trade. This postcard was sent by a lady on a trip to Barnard Castle with the 'Mothers' of Albert Road Spiritualist Church, Blackpool. The building was demolished in the 1980s.

Leck church, 22 October 1913. Just before midnight on 21 October 1913 a fire broke out in the chancel which by 3 a.m. had completely gutted the church. This photograph looks down the nave to the tower at the west end. Note the bell which had fallen from the belfry.

St Peter's, Leck, 22 October 1913. The fire was so fierce that some of the stone pillars crumbled away to a third of their former circumference; this can clearly be seen in this photograph. Commenting on the causes of the fire which destroyed Leck church, the *Lancaster Guardian* pointed out that although some people attributed it to lightning the more probable cause was the church lighting, consisting of oil lamps and candles. It is probably not a coincidence that during the previous evening the choir had been practising in the chancel where the fire broke out. Leck was part of the parish of St John the Baptist, Tunstall, and a chapel of ease had existed here for many years. It was too small to accommodate all the pupils of the Clergy Daughters' School established at Cowan Bridge from 1824. During Charlotte Brontë's stay there she and the older girls had to attend Sunday services at Tunstall, but after 1825 the chapel was extended and all the girls were accommodated at Leck until the school moved to Casterton in 1833. In 1878 it was rebuilt by Paley & Austin of Lancaster at a cost of £4,000.

Leck Church, *c.* 1932. St Peter's was rebuilt by Paley & Austin in 1915 and all traces of that disastrous fire were removed.

Leck Hall, *c.* 1908. The 4th Lord Shuttleworth of Barbon Manor and Gawthorpe Hall bought the house in 1953 from a distant cousin, David Henley-Welch, and proceeded to demolish a redundant office wing. It is now the Shuttleworths' main residence, as they gave Gawthorpe to the National Trust in 1972.

Leck Hall, *c.* 1900. This neo-classical house was built a hundred years previously by the Welch family to the designs of John Webb. In 1900 Henry Thomas Welch would have been living here. His son Edward, who died in 1926, was the last of the family in the direct line.

Melling, *c.* 1912. The village street, then as now, was the main road between Lancaster and Kirkby Lonsdale. Looking south, the vicarage gates are on the immediate left with the tower of St Wilfrid's Church rising behind. An early fourteenth-century building with a fifteenth-century tower rising 55 ft, the church was enlarged in the eighteenth century and restored in 1856 by E.G. Paley of Lancaster. In 1895 the Revd William Grenside re-introduced the ancient dedication of St Wilfrid, which had somehow slipped into that of St Peter during the Reformation. The large Victorian house in the centre of this photograph has the date 1878 carved on to the porch and stands next to two seventeenth-century cottages. Set back from the road, on the right, is Swallow's Nest cottage with a workman on a ladder in front of an upper window.

Canon William Grenside (1821–1913), Melling Vicarage, 1905. Canon Grenside was photographed on the steps of the vicarage, with St Wilfrid's Church behind, on the fiftieth anniversary of his induction as Vicar of Melling in 1855 and the year in which he was made an Honorary Canon of Manchester Cathedral. He rebuilt and enlarged the vicarage and restored the church. As a friend of John Ruskin, whose ideas regarding the spritual integrity of medieval art and architecture greatly influenced him, he attempted a thorough restoration of St Wilfrid's which involved stripping away many of its post-Reformation accretions. This was so prolonged and ruthless that the churchwardens felt obliged to record that they required notice of any change to the fabric of the building. Instead he refurnished the church to the designs of Paley & Austin and raised the sanctuary by the addition of an extra step in black marble, and lined its walls with pink-veined marble. (see also p. 156.)

Swallow's Nest, Melling, *c.* 1912. Canon Grenside bought this row of three cottages and prepared the central one – Swallow's Nest – for his retirement. As he died in 1913 at the age of ninety-one, still Vicar of Melling, it was not clear when he intended this to be. His arms and motto – *Benedictus benedicat* 'blessing on the blessed', are carved over the doorway beneath the segmental pediment. To the left is Swallow's Nest Cottage, to the right Rose Cottage.

School house, Melling, *c.* 1906. Melling Endowed School was founded in the early eighteenth century in this building set on the edge of Melling Moor. In 1844 a new schoolhouse was erected nearby, overlooking the Wennington road, and this became a dwelling for a master and schoolmistress. At the turn of the century these were William Hartley and his wife Hannah.

Melling station, 1930s. On 10 April 1867 the Furness & Midland Joint Railway was opened between Wennington and Carnforth connecting the West Riding of Yorkshire with Barrow-in-Furness. Melling was one of three new stations on this line, opening for passenger traffic on 6 June. It was closed by British Rail on 12 September 1960.

Foster's Arms Hotel, Wennington, 1907. John Foster of Bradford bought Hornby Castle estate in 1860 which included the hotel at Wennington managed by Mrs Margaret Coates, also listed in trade directories as a farmer. This large establishment catered for travellers on the Lancaster–Skipton railway line which opened in 1849.

Wennington Bridge, *c.* 1925. The Lancaster–Wennington section of the North Western Railway's line to Skipton was completed in October 1849. The first passenger service ran on 17 November, with a connecting horse-drawn omnibus to take passengers from Wennington to Clapham (which was the closest the line, still being built, approached from the other direction). On 2 May 1850 a new permanent station opened at its present site, replacing a temporary building ¾ of a mile to the west. The bridge connecting the station to the village was rebuilt and made considerably wider at about this time. The completed line was opened on 1 June 1850 and shortly afterwards transferred to the Midland Railway which, together with the Furness Railway, opened a connecting line to Carnforth in 1867. The stationmaster, William Hanley, retired on 8 June 1907 and was succeeded by James Garner. The bulk of the Foster's Arms Hotel can be seen across the River Wenning, with the rest of the village centre to the right.

Wennington, *c.* 1925. The enclosure beneath the parapet of the bridge is a pinfold, used to gather sheep or cattle together. The post office and grocer's shop, for many years run by the Middleton family, is directly ahead. The figure in the doorway is possibly Mary Middleton. Mill Farm, one of a number of farmhouses clustering around the village centre, is on the far right facing the road to Low Bentham.

Wennington, 1930s. The road east to Low Bentham narrows considerably after passing through a large open space at the centre of the village, with buildings encroaching on the road after it passes Mill Farm (right). This is common in villages accustomed to holding fairs or cattle markets and enables the road to be easily closed to contain livestock.

The Wennington Arch, *c.* 1924. It simply marked the boundary of the townships of Melling and Wennington on the main road. Only the lower three courses of the left-hand pillar and the gateway remain today, the rest having been removed to accommodate traffic wider than a single governess cart.

Wennington Hall, *c.* 1910. The Manor of Wennington descended through the Wennington and Morley families until sold in 1674 to Henry Marsden. His descendant, John Marsden, bought Hornby Castle in 1789 and sold Wennington Hall to Robert Hesketh of Heysham and Rossall. Sir Peter Hesketh Fleetwood, the founder of the town of Fleetwood, was born in the old hall in 1801.

Wennington Hall, *c.* 1910. Richard Saunders bought the Wennington Hall Estate in 1841, but it was left to his son William to build the present hall in 1855. He employed the Lancaster architect E.G. Paley to design the house in a Tudor-Gothic style, perhaps as a conscious reference to the medieval ancestors of his wife, Dorothy Morley, who had once owned Wennington. Their son, Charles Morley Saunders, is included in the group photograph of members of the Lunesdale Gun Club. His niece, Florence Hope, married Eric Lees of Thurland Castle, son of Colonel and Mrs Lees. William Morley Saunders, Charles' son, sold the Hall in 1939. It was bought on behalf of the Greycoat Fellowship as a guest house for the unemployed. In 1955 it became a boarding school for maladjusted boys.

St Michael the Archangel, Whittington, *c.* 1810. This engraving shows the church, dating back to 1291, before the drastic 1875 rebuilding. However fanciful the classically inspired figures in the lower right-hand corner, seen drawing water from a well, the spring does exist and is marked today by an old disused water pump.

Whittington church, *c.* 1910. The church was restored in 1841 and in 1875 it was gothicized, original medieval detailing often giving way to Victorian copies. This view was taken from the footpath crossing the rector's glebe land and Whittington Hall Park to the village.

Whittington Rectory, *c.* 1910. Built in 1728 by the then Rector, the Revd George Hornby, it stands to the east of the church. The Revd William Carus-Wilson became Rector of Whittington from 1825 but resigned in 1834 having built his own church at Casterton.

Whittington church, 1940s. Seen from the footpath crossing Whittington Hall Park to the village, the churchyard has not yet been extended into the rector's glebe land. To the right of the porch stands the war memorial, a cross of Stainton limestone which was unveiled by Lord Shuttleworth, Lord Lieutenant of Lancashire on 31 October 1920.

Whittington Boys' School, *c.* 1904. Eleanor, the sender of this postcard, wrote that 'this picture was once the boys school at Whittington but is now no more'. In 1761 William Margisson left £320 in trust, the interest to provide for the poor and endow a school for their children. Thomas Greenwood from Box Tree, Lupton, was taught here before leaving in 1771 to learn navigation at Kellet School. The following year, at the age of fourteen, he began a six-year apprenticeship at sea out of the port of Lancaster, eventually rising to the rank of captain. During an eventful career he crossed the Atlantic 101 times. The school's most famous pupil was William Sturgeon, born at Whittington in 1783, who also left at the age of thirteen to take up an apprenticeship to a shoemaker. Later, during a career as a gunner in the artillery, he acquired sufficent knowledge of practical science to become, by 1824, a lecturer in science and philosophy at the military college in Woolwich. Among his discoveries were the soft-iron electromagnet, amalgamated zinc battery and electromagnetic coil machine. Strangley enough, he has no memorial in Whittington. In 1875 H. Aylmer Greene of Whittington Hall built the co-educational village school, making the boys' school building redundant.

Church tower, Whittington, 1930s. The tower is the oldest part of the church to have escaped the drastic restoration of 1875. Built in the late fifteenth century, it stands 50 ft high. In the niche half-way up is a statue of the good shepherd, probably dating from the time of the restoration.

Whittington, 1940s. This is the road from Burton-in-Kendal and Hutton Roof looking east. Hidden among the trees to the right is the church.

The Village. Whittington.

Whittington, late 1930s. This is the main street facing north, along which the Royal Hotel omnibus from Kirkby Lonsdale used to travel to meet every train stopping at Arkholme station. The building with a flagpole (left) is the village school, erected in 1875 by H. Aylmer Greene at a cost of £4,000 to take up to 120 pupils. He was the youngest son of Thomas Greene, MP for Lancaster 1824–57, who bought Whittington Hall in 1830 and rebuilt it to the designs of George Webster of Kendal between 1831 and 1836. The Dragon's Head Private Hotel and Inn, called the Rose Tree until the turn of the century, is set back from the road to the right. The sign at the end of Tithebarn Cottage indicates its position. The house with a porch, next but one to the end of the row, was the village post office. Directly outside stands a telegraph pole with 'Telephone' sign, and a little further on, a baker's van has stopped by the side of the road.

Whittington, 1930s. This unknown farmer, holding a feed bucket for the horse, is said to have farmed in the area around Whittington.

Newton Hall, *c.* 1907. North North (see p. 152) employed Paley & Austin to renovate Thurland Castle after the fire of 1876 and also rebuild Newton Hall in a Jacobethan style in 1880. In 1885 he sold the castle and came to live here. He died in 1910 and was succeeded by his son Brigadier General Bordrigge North North, High Sheriff of Westmorland in 1907.

ARKHOLME

Village crossroads, *c.* 1913. On the left is the post office and shop belonging to Mark Ireland, who was listed as sub-master, stationer, boot, shoe and clog maker and parish clerk in 1913. His father, John Ireland, had been sub-postmaster and shoemaker here until the 1880s when his wife Ellen took charge, handing over to their son by 1901. Mark's older brother, Alfred, had already set up in business as sub-postmaster and shoemaker at Cowan Bridge. A little further on, the main road from Kirkby Lonsdale to Carnforth passes across the top of Arkholme village street. On the other side, directly ahead, is the smithy built by James Yates in about 1817; and standing forward of the other cottages, a water pump can clearly be seen against its whitewashed walls. Christopher Bibby was the blacksmith at this time, paying ground rent to Mrs Clough until 1922 and thereafter to the sons of Dr Paget-Tomlinson of The Biggins. To the right is the Bay Horse Hotel, whose landlord was Richard Metcalfe. The wall in the right foreground encloses the National School, endowed in 1851 by Mary and Eliza Cort in memory of their father the Revd Robert Cort, Curate of Arkholme 1792–3. It was built in 1867–8 for £540, including the master's house, and enlarged in 1900.

Village crossroads, *c.* 1930. This is roughly the same view as the previous postcard but with some changes. For example, the shop and post office has moved next door and there is a telephone box outside. Across the main road is the newly built parish hall, whose door faces down the street.

The police station, *c.* 1927. The village constable was housed in the middle of a row of cottages facing the main road south to Storrs Hall and Carnforth. In 1907, 64-year old Francis Pearson of Storrs Hall, riding down this road to the village in the dark, was badly injured when his bicycle hit a pot hole.

Views of Arkholme, pre-1914. Although mixed farming was far more common at this time, the Lune Valley was – and still is – a pastoral region engaged primarily in sheep farming, dairying and beef production. Arkholme was a typical rural village, home to a number of solid and respectable labourers and small farmers, although the agricultural depression at the end of the nineteenth century had significantly reduced the population of the village to around 250.

The main street of Arkholme looking west, *c.* 1910. Pevsner described it as 'a very pretty street'. Architecturally it is full of interest with many solid rural houses and farm buildings. Many of them were occupied by tradesmen including basket-makers, a craft particularly associated with Arkholme and dating from at least the early eighteenth century. Acres of osiers (willow rods) were grown in the fertile fields beside the River Lune. The Irelands were the most prominent basket-making family and for much of the time probably pursued the craft along with farming and other occupations. By 1841 there were eleven basket-makers in Arkholme supplying a variety of wares, especially baskets for potato farmers in the Fylde and for cockle-fishers around Morecambe Bay. From the 1860s there was a decline and the last active basket-maker was Charlie Ireland who died in 1959.

Cruck Cottage, Arkholme, now demolished, represented a type of building once common in many Lune Valley villages. Cruck-framed houses used pairs of vertical inclined timbers, usually curved (or crooked), spaced at intervals to support the roof timbers. The roof thatch is probably of rye-straw, the toughest variety, which lasted around thirty years. Also widespread were stone-flagged roofs of local carboniferous sandstone seen on the projecting wing. The great weight and size of the stone slates determined the shallow pitch of the roof. The solid, sturdy appearance of these buildings and the local materials used in their construction placed them in harmony with the local landscape and made them highly attractive.

The Vicarage, *c.* 1909. Arkholme was part of the parish of St Wilfrid's, Melling, until 1866 when it became a separate parish. A new vicarage was built to the south of the village street and here Mark Ireland, the village sub-postmaster (left), can be seen standing in its garden. In 1909 the Revd William Shepherd was the resident curate.

Cawood House, *c.* 1905. Built in 1748, probably by the Smith family, it was restored and enlarged earlier this century. A little further behind stands Carus House, primarily Jacobean but with a Georgian façade added by William Turner Carus. This has since been demolished and replaced by a modern housing development.

The parish church, *c.* 1918, which originated as a chapel of ease of the parish of St Wilfrid's, Melling. Built in the fifteenth century, the bellcote dates from 1788 while the porch and windows are Austin & Paley additions of 1897. The mound behind the church was once part of a motte-and-bailey defensive work guarding a crossing of the Lune.

Church interior, 1907. During the Austin & Paley restoration of 1897 the sanctuary was extended 15½ ft eastwards to create a chancel and the high-backed pews and triple-decker pulpit were removed. Decorated as if for a flower festival, the sanctuary is without the panelling that now lines its walls. To the left is the organ built by Bibby & Wolfenden in 1906 and dedicated on 19 May. Richard Bibby of Caulking House, Arkholme, was listed in the local trade directories as a cabinet-maker, joiner and wheelwright in 1898 and 1901; by 1905 he was described as an organ builder. John Wolfenden, on the other hand, was described as a pianoforte tuner of 19 Main Street, Kirkby Lonsdale, until the First World War and briefly, in 1906, as an organ builder. It would seem that the partnership was short-lived. Certainly a large part of the Bibby family emigrated to New Zealand in 1909.

The ferry, *c.* 1905. The Lune is fordable at this point, accounting for Arkholme's position on the river opposite Melling. The ferryman – here Thomas Ireland, a basket-maker of Boat House – provided an easier and quicker crossing for a small charge. During the flood of 3 November 1927 this stretch of the Lune was over a mile wide.

Storrs Hall, *c.* 1905. Francis Pearson, a Kirkby Lonsdale solicitor known as the 'Kirkby Devil', bought the hall in 1848. He rebuilt and extended the house in 1850, adding the tower on the left, probably to the designs of George Webster of Kendal.

Storrs Hall, *c.* 1908. The 'Kirkby Devil's' arms and motto – *Malgre le tort*, 'in spite of fault', so suitable for a solicitor – are carved above the door together with the marital initials. In 1820 he founded a successful legal practice in Kirkby Lonsdale which his two sons carried on after his death in 1859. His elder son, also called Francis, succeeded to Storrs Hall; Alexander, the youngest, inherited Lune Cottage, Kirkby Lonsdale, from an uncle, which his son Alexander Pearson, the historian, renamed Abbot's Brow. Francis died in 1910, having retired from the family firm of Pearson & Pearson in 1895. His son, also Francis and a solicitor, inherited the family home but preferred to live at Brant Howe, Kirkby Lonsdale, renting the hall out until his death in 1917. Storrs was sold in the 1950s by Sir Francis Pearson, formerly a Parliamentary Private Secretary to the Prime Minister Sir Alec Douglas-Home, who moved to Gressingham Hall.

Arkholme Trinity fête, 1909. The village fête was held on Trinity Sunday at Storrs Hall in the year before Francis Pearson died. The death of his son Francis in 1917 caused a financial crisis in the family and Brant Howe was sold. His widow went to live at Poole House in the village.

Arkholme station, c. 1906. The Furness & Midland Joint Railway opened between Wennington and Carnforth in 1867 with a station at Arkholme, on the main road to Kirkby Lonsdale. This became one of the two most convenient stations for the town, the Royal Hotel omnibus meeting every train which stopped here. This photograph was taken from the road bridge facing west.

Lord Henry C. Bentinck receiving
H.R.H. Princess Christian at Arkholme,
April 27th, 1906.

On 27 April 1906 HRH Princess Christian of Schleswig-Holstein, third daughter of Queen Victoria, arrived at Arkholme station en route to Kirkby Lonsdale where she was to stay at Lunefield as a guest of the Countess of Bective. The Princess, having alighted from the royal train, is seen here being greeted by Lord Henry Cavendish-Bentinck of Underley Hall, son-in-law of Lady Bective. When the train departed they had to make their way across the railway line to the station building (right), there being no footbridge. The stationmaster, Robert Teale, resplendent in his uniform, is seen waiting on the far platform with a loyal reception committee.

Arkholme station, 1930s. The station was opened for goods traffic on 10 April 1867 and passenger traffic on 6 June. It was closed on 12 September 1960, together with Borwick and Melling stations on the same line. The buildings incorporate a stationmaster's house (left) and offices (right).

TUNSTALL

These two cottages, directly opposite the Fenwick Arms, had recently been joined together. One of the ladies in the doorway is Annie and the three children are Elsie, Nancy and Amy, only just returned from school when this photograph was taken by W.H. Berry in about 1907. Berry, a photographer and stationer of Kirkby Lonsdale, seems to have visited Tunstall frequently at this time, taking the following two photographs which he published as postcards.

The main road through Tunstall from Melling to Kirkby Lonsdale, looking north, *c.* 1905. On the left is the Fenwick Arms Inn & Private Hotel (the Fenwick family owned Burrow Hall and estate) whose landlord in 1907 was Richard T. Yates, farmer and village blacksmith.

Village street, *c.* 1907, with the Fenwick Arms to the right. The village post office, with a sign above the door, is on the left next to the cottage shown on the opposite page. Henry Shepherd was the sub-postmaster and grocer for the village.

St John the Baptist's Church, *c. 1906*. The Revd William Carus-Wilson, Vicar of Tunstall 1816–1825,
founded the Clergy Daughters' School at Cowan Bridge in 1823 and required its pupils to attend Sunday
services at the church. Charlotte Brontë, a pupil from 1824–5, incorporated memories of this into her
novel *Jane Eyre*: 'We had to walk two miles to Brocklebridge Church, where our patron officiated. We set
out cold, we arrived at church colder: during morning service we became almost paralyzed. It was too far
to return to dinner, and an allowance of cold meat and bread, in the same penurious proportion observed
in our ordinary meals, was served round between the services. At the close of the afternoon service we
returned by an exposed and hilly road, where the bitter winter wind, blowing over a range of snowy
summits to the north, almost flayed the skin from our faces.' The thirteenth-century church was rebuilt in
the fifteenth century and a two-storey porch added. It was in the upper room that the Clergy Daughters'
School girls ate their midday meal. At the time this would have been reached by way of a gallery, removed
in 1847. In keeping with John Ruskin's views on restoration, the church has retained its fifteenth-century
windows intact, possibly because of his friendship and influence with the Lees of Thurland Castle.

St John the Baptist, east end, *c.* 1930. The church gates and posts were given by Mrs Eliza Nutter and her pupils at Cantsfield Cottage. Before her marriage Mrs Nutter taught at the Clergy Daughters' School. This postcard was published by Alfred Ireland, sub-postmaster at Cowan Bridge.

Thurland Castle, Tunstall, 1853. Richard Toulmin North employed Jeffry Wyatt (later Sir Jeffry Wyattville, George IV's architect at Windsor Castle 1824–37) to renovate his ruinous medieval castle in 1809–10. This fanciful neo-Gothic creation is the result, although Francis Webster of Kendal extended the east wing (right) in 1829. The romantic feeling is enhanced by the reinstated moat fed by Cant Beck.

Thurland Castle from the north. In 1865 North Burton inherited his great-uncle's Thurland Castle estate and adopted his surname, becoming North North. The tower in the centre foreground, together with the wing, to the left, extending back from it as far as the third block of chimneys, is a refaced part of the original medieval castle. Continuing further back still is the Francis Webster addition of 1829. The north wing to the right of the medieval work, as far as the tower, is Jeffrey Wyatt's work of 1809–10. After the

1876 fire, Paley & Austin of Lancaster made significant exterior and interior alterations, adding the rest of the north wing, outbuildings and stables to the right. Halfway up the terrace on the left is a doorway against which the group photograph with Colonel and Mrs Lees was taken (see p. 156).

Thurland Castle from the south. After the fire of 17 April 1876, in which most of the early nineteenth-century work was lost, Paley & Austin were employed to restore the damaged rooms and make alterations in an Elizabethan style. This included building the enclosing wall to the courtyard and the entrance gate, where a medieval gateway had stood before demolition in 1829.

Thurland Castle from the south, *c.* 1906. In 1885 North North sold the castle to Lieutenant-Colonel Edward Brown Lees, a colliery owner from Oldham. He proceeded to engage Paley, Austin & Paley to continue the programme of alterations, unifying the disparate collection of buildings and adding a billiard room, library, stables and outbuildings in 1888–9.

Dora Lees at Thurland Castle, *c.* 1888. Born in Blackburn in 1846, she married Edward Lees in 1877. She was one of the girls to whom John Ruskin wrote his Winnington Letters, so-called after the school she attended in Cheshire during the early 1860s. They maintained a lifelong friendship, the Lees often visiting Ruskin at his Brantwood home. After Colonel Lees bought the castle and manor of Tunstall in 1885 she devoted much time to her duties as chatelaine. She died in 1912, sixteen years after her husband. Their son, Ronald, Vicar of Tunstall, sold the estate in 1938.

Group photograph on the terrace, Thurland Castle, 1893. Left to right: Dora Lees; Arthur Severn, son of Keats' friend Joseph Severn; Joan Severn, Ruskin's cousin and heir, married to Arthur; the Revd William Grenside, Vicar of Melling; and Edward Lees. Through Ruskin, the Lees became friends with Arthur and Joan Severn who lived at Brantwood where Joan acted as housekeeper for her cousin. Mr Grenside was another friend of Ruskin, who is said to have been influenced by him in the reordering of St Wilfrid's Church, Melling. Unfortunately, by 1893 Ruskin's mental illness had taken a deep hold and he rarely recognized either his surroundings or his friends.

Greta Bridge. The River Greta, which flows off Ingleborough and Blea Moor into the Lune below Tunstall, is capable of inflicting great damage in times of flood. This bridge, which carries the main road north from Lancaster, has been rebuilt many times. The postcard (above), published by W.H. Berry in about 1905, looks north to a row of cottages, now demolished, on the edge of Thurland Castle park. The view of the bridge (below) was taken from the west in about 1930.

ACKNOWLEDGEMENTS

The photographs in this volume have been amassed over a number of years and from a variety of sources. Special thanks must go to Lancaster City Museums and the public libraries in Kendal (Local Studies Collection) and Lancaster (Reference Library) for permission to reproduce photographs and for the helpfulness of their staff. We are grateful to the following individuals for advice, information and the loan of images in a most unselfish manner:

Robert Alston, Susan Ashworth, Malcolm Davies, William Dennison, Peter Donnelly, Stuart Eastwood, S. French, Michael Gibson, Miss M.I. Huggonson, W.P. Howson, Leslie Leak, John M. MacKenzie, Don Potter, Kevin Ramsdale, Garnett Richardson, Audrey Phillips, Ron Severs, William Snowley, Miss M. Wright.

BRITAIN IN OLD PHOTOGRAPHS

Lincoln
Lincoln Cathedral
The Lincolnshire Coast
Liverpool
Around Llandudno
Around Lochaber
Theatrical London
Around Louth
The Lower Fal Estuary
Lowestoft
Luton
Lympne Airfield
Lytham St Annes
Maidenhead
Around Maidenhead
Around Malvern
Manchester
Manchester Road & Rail
Mansfield
Marlborough: A Second Selection
Marylebone & Paddington
Around Matlock
Melton Mowbray
Around Melksham
The Mendips
Merton & Morden
Middlesbrough
Midsomer Norton & Radstock
Around Mildenhall
Milton Keynes
Minehead
Monmouth & the River Wye
The Nadder Valley
Newark
Around Newark
Newbury
Newport, Isle of Wight
The Norfolk Broads
Norfolk at War
North Fylde
North Lambeth
North Walsham & District
Northallerton
Northampton
Around Norwich
Nottingham 1944–74
The Changing Face of Nottingham
Victorian Nottingham
Nottingham Yesterday & Today
Nuneaton
Around Oakham
Ormskirk & District
Otley & District
Oxford: The University
Oxford Yesterday & Today
Oxfordshire Railways: A Second
  Selection
Oxfordshire at School
Around Padstow
Pattingham & Wombourne

Penwith
Penzance & Newlyn
Around Pershore
Around Plymouth
Poole
Portsmouth
Poulton-le-Fylde
Preston
Prestwich
Pudsey
Radcliffe
RAF Chivenor
RAF Cosford
RAF Hawkinge
RAF Manston
RAF Manston: A Second Selection
RAF St Mawgan
RAF Tangmere
Ramsgate & Thanet Life
Reading
Reading: A Second Selection
Redditch & the Needle District
Redditch: A Second Selection
Richmond, Surrey
Rickmansworth
Around Ripley
The River Soar
Romney Marsh
Romney Marsh: A Second
  Selection
Rossendale
Around Rotherham
Rugby
Around Rugeley
Ruislip
Around Ryde
St Albans
St Andrews
Salford
Salisbury
Salisbury: A Second Selection
Salisbury: A Third Selection
Around Salisbury
Sandhurst & Crowthorne
Sandown & Shanklin
Sandwich
Scarborough
Scunthorpe
Seaton, Lyme Regis & Axminster
Around Seaton & Sidmouth
Sedgley & District
The Severn Vale
Sherwood Forest
Shrewsbury
Shrewsbury: A Second Selection
Shropshire Railways
Skegness
Around Skegness
Skipton & the Dales
Around Slough

Smethwick
Somerton & Langport
Southampton
Southend-on-Sea
Southport
Southwark
Southwell
Southwold to Aldeburgh
Stafford
Around Stafford
Staffordshire Railways
Around Staveley
Stepney
Stevenage
The History of Stilton Cheese
Stoke-on-Trent
Stoke Newington
Stonehouse to Painswick
Around Stony Stratford
Around Stony Stratford: A Second
  Selection
Stowmarket
Streatham
Stroud & the Five Valleys
Stroud & the Five Valleys: A
  Second Selection
Stroud's Golden Valley
The Stroudwater and Thames &
  Severn Canals
The Stroudwater and Thames &
  Severn Canals: A Second
  Selection
Suffolk at Work
Suffolk at Work: A Second
  Selection
The Heart of Suffolk
Sunderland
Sutton
Swansea
Swindon: A Third Selection
Swindon: A Fifth Selection
Around Tamworth
Taunton
Around Taunton
Teesdale
Teesdale: A Second Selection
Tenbury Wells
Around Tettenhall & Codshall
Tewkesbury & the Vale of
  Gloucester
Thame to Watlington
Around Thatcham
Around Thirsk
Thornbury to Berkeley
Tipton
Around Tonbridge
Trowbridge
Around Truro
TT Races
Tunbridge Wells

Tunbridge Wells: A Second
  Selection
Twickenham
Uley, Dursley & Cam
The Upper Fal
The Upper Tywi Valley
Uxbridge, Hillingdon & Cowley
The Vale of Belvoir
The Vale of Conway
Ventnor
Wakefield
Wallingford
Walsall
Waltham Abbey
Wandsworth at War
Wantage, Faringdon & the Vale
  Villages
Around Warwick
Weardale
Weardale: A Second Selection
Wednesbury
Wells
Welshpool
West Bromwich
West Wight
Weston-super-Mare
Around Weston-super-Mare
Weymouth & Portland
Around Wheatley
Around Whetstone
Whitchurch to Market Drayton
Around Whitstable
Wigton & the Solway Plain
Willesden
Around Wilton
Wimbledon
Around Windsor
Wingham, Addisham &
  Littlebourne
Wisbech
Witham & District
Witney
Around Witney
The Witney District
Wokingham
Around Woodbridge
Around Woodstock
Woolwich
Woolwich Royal Arsenal
Around Wootton Bassett,
  Cricklade & Purton
Worcester
Worcester in a Day
Around Worcester
Worcestershire at Work
Around Worthing
Wotton-under-Edge to Chipping
  Sodbury
Wymondham & Attleborough
The Yorkshire Wolds